This book offers a new theory of proper names and a new view of the nature of necessity. It features analyses of the concept of a physical thing and the relation between the names of things and the things they name. It questions the prevalent view that names "refer to" or "denote" the things they name. Instead, it presents a theory of proper names, according to which names express certain special properties that the things they name exhibit. This theory leads to some important conclusions about whether things have any of their properties as a matter of necessity.

This will be an important book for philosophers in metaphysics and the philosophy of language, though it will also interest linguists concerned with the semantics of natural language.

CAMBRIDGE STUDIES IN PHILOSOPHY

Ontology, Modality, and the Fallacy of Reference

CAMBRIDGE STUDIES IN PHILOSOPHY

FLINT SCHIER *Deeper into pictures*
ANTHONY APPIAH *Assertion and conditionals*
ROBERT BROWN *Analyzing love*
ROBERT M. GORDON *The structure of emotions*
FRANÇOIS RECANATI *Meaning and force*
WILLIAM G. LYCAN *Judgement and justification*
GERALD DWORKIN *The theory and practice of autonomy*
MICHAEL TYE *The metaphysics of mind*
DAVID O. BRINK *Moral realism and the foundations of ethics*
W. D. HART *Engines of the soul*
PAUL K. MOSER *Knowledge and evidence*
D. M. ARMSTRONG *A combinatorial theory of possibility*
JOHN BISHOP *Natural agency*
CHRISTOPHER J. MALONEY *The mundane matter of the mental language*
GERALD GAUS *Value and justification*
CARL GINET *On action*
MARK RICHARD *Propositional attitudes*
MARK HELLER *The ontology of physical objects*
JOHN BIGELOW and ROBERT PARGETTER *Science and necessity*
CHRISTOPHER S. HILL *Sensations*
CONRAD D. JOHNSON *Moral legislation*
FRANCIS SNARE *Morals, motive, and convention*
JOHN HEIL *The nature of true minds*
ANDREW NEWMAN *The physical basis of predication*
DAVID OWENS *Causes and coincidences*

Ontology, Modality, and the Fallacy of Reference

Michael Jubien
University of California – Davis

CAMBRIDGE UNIVERSITY PRESS
Cambridge, New York, Melbourne, Madrid, Cape Town, Singapore, São Paulo, Delhi

Cambridge University Press
The Edinburgh Building, Cambridge CB2 8RU, UK

Published in the United States of America by Cambridge University Press, New York

www.cambridge.org
Information on this title: www.cambridge.org/9780521108577

First published 1993
This digitally printed version 2009

A catalogue record for this publication is available from the British Library

Library of Congress Cataloguing in Publication data

Jubien, Michael.

Ontology, modality, and the fallacy of reference / Michael Jubien.

p. cm. – (Cambridge studies in philosophy)

Includes bibliographical references.

ISBN 0-521-43399-1 (hc)

1. Reference (Philosophy) 2. Names. 3. Identity. 4. Essence (Philosophy) 5. Necessity (Philosophy) 6. Ontology. 7. Modality (Logic) I. Title. II. Series.

B105.R25J83 1993

121′.68 – dc20 92-33790
CIP

ISBN 978-0-521-43399-0 hardback
ISBN 978-0-521-10857-7 paperback

For Sidney

Contents

Preface

Saul Kripke gave three lectures on naming and necessity at Princeton in January of 1970. I had the good fortune to hear them, and I've spent a good deal of time thinking about the topics ever since.

For the past few years I have also thought about the concept of a *thing*. During this period it became increasingly clear to me that how we think about what it is to be a thing has a profound effect on how we should think about naming and necessity. In this book I suggest a way of thinking about things, and draw a number of conclusions about naming and necessity. Several of these conclusions may be surprising. For example I will defend each of the following claims.

1. Mereological essentialism – the doctrine that things have their parts essentially – is true.
2. Ordinary proper names are *not* "rigid designators." In fact they aren't designators *at all*.
3. Both direct-reference and definite-description theories of proper names are wrong.
4. Ordinary examples of "identity statements" are *not* identity statements (but genuine identity statements *are* necessary truths).
5. Typical examples of "*de re* necessary truths" are actually false.
6. The usual way of characterizing *essentialism*, in terms of the scopes of modal operators, misses its intuitive mark. Despite this, the intuitions that led philosophers like Saul Kripke and Ruth Marcus to essentialism are generally right.

In connection with Theses 2–4, I will offer what I think is a brand new theory of names. In connection with Theses 5 and 6, I will propose a new characterization of *essentialism*, one that I think fits naturally with familiar essentialist intuitions about cases, once they are properly understood.

I will maintain in this book that we have all been victims of a certain misunderstanding of how *reference* and *identity* are related. I call this misunderstanding the *Fallacy of Reference*. Thus I will be urging that we abandon a way of thinking that is so deeply ingrained that my opposing it may even be thought absurd or self-refuting. I ask the reader not to jump to this conclusion, but instead to step back and take the idea seriously. I think many benefits accompany a recognition of the fallacy for what it is, not the least of which is avoiding the philosophical chaos it has so far produced. Avoiding the fallacy is intimately involved in arriving at Theses 2–5.

The literature on the various topics treated in this book is extensive and often very complicated. I have made no effort to provide an overview. I am sure that many things have been said on these topics that are overlooked in what follows. (It may also be that some of the things I say have been said before without my knowledge.)

I presented some of this material at the APA – Pacific meetings in Los Angeles in 1990. Nathan Salmon was commentator and I thank him for his remarks. Some of the material was also presented at Arizona State University in 1990 and at the University of California, Irvine, in 1992. I am grateful for a number of helpful comments. I have also presented the material here at the University of California, Davis, more than once. Many graduate students and colleagues, from Davis and elsewhere, have offered helpful comments. These include George Bealer, David Copp, David Cowles, Fred Feldman, Greg Fitch, Joel Friedman, Richard Healey, Dennis Holden, Jeffrey King, G. J. Mattey, Terence Parsons, Paul Teller, Michael Wedin, Greg Ray, Tony Roy, Cranston Paull, Melinda Campbell, Beth Forrester, Robert Mutti, Alison McIntosh, Bill Hirstein, Richard Schubert, Ronald Pritchard, Leslie Stapp, and two anonymous readers for Cambridge University Press. I am grateful to them all, and to any others I may have forgotten to mention. I am extremely indebted to my wife, Sidney Mannheim Jubien, for her comments and for her warm support. I owe a large general philosophical debt to Saul Kripke, and I will be pleased if that shows in what follows.

Davis, California

1

Ontology

The goal of this brief chapter is to present a number of ontological claims and presuppositions that will play a central role in the remainder of the book. The main topics are the nature of *things*; the existence of *properties, relations*, and *propositions*; and the metaphor of *possible worlds*.

1. THINGS

In this section I want to present a certain "naturalistic" view about the contents of the physical world – a view about what (physical) *things* (or *objects*) the world contains. This view may be crudely characterized by the mysterious-sounding claim that, in a certain sense, *there are no things*, but, partly as a consequence, there are as many things as we like.

A slightly better characterization of the first part of the claim is that the world does not come *naturally* divided into a definite array of discrete things. Instead, it consists of "stuff" spread more or less unevenly and more or less densely around space-time. From within our own – forgive me – "conceptual scheme," the stuff occupying one spatiotemporal region will be taken as constituting a thing, while the stuff occupying another such region will not. But carving the world into things *our* way (pretending for a moment that we actually do this in some unique way) is *not* compelled by features intrinsic to the distribution of stuff that confronts us. It may be true that, given the way we are (especially given how we are equipped to interact with the confronting distribution), carving up the world the way we do is somehow optimal, or generally advantageous, or whatever. But such a fact would not *just* be one about the intrinsic character of the distribution of stuff outside us.

So I am taking it as a fundamental ontological doctrine that the raw material of the physical universe is *stuff*, not *things*, and that the organization of (some or all of) this stuff into things is done by *us*. I will not argue directly for this view, nor will I attempt to define the term 'stuff'. In particular, I will not have anything to say about the *physical* nature of stuff, nor will I take a position on such questions as how many different *kinds* of stuff there are. Instead I will take the notion of stuff as primitive, and will try to motivate the view simply by explaining it a little more carefully.

The fact that we view the planet Mars as a single thing but do not view the "mereological sum" of Mars and the moon as a single thing is just that: a fact about *how we view* the stuff occupying certain regions. There are no underlying facts, strictly about these regions and their contents, that *determine* that there is a single thing encompassing all (or very nearly all) of the stuff in one of the regions but there is no single thing with this property in the other. It is nevertheless true that if there had been no intelligent life, but the universe was otherwise pretty much as it is, there would have been a roughly spherical thing where Mars actually is. For, in describing that possibility, we are entitled to the full resources of *our* language, so it is legitimate for us to describe it as containing a roughly spherical *thing*. (In fact it would be the planet Mars.) But there are countless other equally legitimate ways of completely and correctly describing the same possibility that do not include the claim that there is a roughly spherical *thing* in that region. Such a description might proceed from a different "conceptual scheme," but it need not. For even *we* may describe the relevant region by saying that a roughly spherical subregion is occupied by stuff of a roughly uniform density near that subregion's surface, which density differs markedly from that of the immediately surrounding subregion, and so forth. Ultimately our description would be complete and correct, though it would not by itself assert the existence of any large spherical *thing*. One moral of this story is that our language is very powerful. It may be an integral part of our conceptual scheme that we view Mars as a single thing, but we are nevertheless able to give physically complete descriptions of states of affairs involving Mars without asserting that Mars is a (single) thing.

None of this really depends on the deservedly notorious notion of a conceptual scheme. What matters is just that it seems clear that beings different from us (or we ourselves) might divide the universe into "things" very differently than we do. In fact there could be intelligent beings who did perfectly well with no "thing" notion at all. I think this humble point is little different from the point that beings a little different from us might divide the color spectrum into major parts in a somewhat different way. Just as experimental psychologists have evidence that the division of the spectrum actually does vary from person to person, metaphysics instructors have evidence that the extension of the word 'thing' varies from person to person. The present point is that variations far more extreme than those we actually encounter are surely possible.

Let us pretend that we actually share a single concept of *being a thing*, and let us call this concept 'ordinary thinghood'. It then appears that ordinary thinghood is not an "intrinsic" property of the stuff of various regions. It is rather a *relational* property: the "projection" obtained by fixing one of the *relata* of a more fundamental *relation* that holds between the stuff of various regions and, for example, ourselves. We may think of this as the *thing-for* (or *thing-with-respect-to*) relation. Then *ordinary thinghood* is the relational property *being a thing for us*. And of course different ways of parametrizing the second *relatum* of the *thing-for* relation will produce different relational "thing" properties of regionalized stuff.

I have just claimed that the *thing-for* relation is more fundamental than the property of *ordinary thinghood*. Let me try to say why, in a rough-and-ready way. I think we have a pretty clear intuition that, for example, the *shorter-than* relation is "more fundamental" than the property *being shorter than Wilt*. There are at least two reasons for this. For one, people could stand in the *relation* even if Wilt did not exist, but surely no one could have the *property* in a world without Wilt. A second and more important consideration is this. Whether a person has the property does not *just* depend on that person's "internal nature." It also depends on Wilt's. I capture this (without offering a definition) by saying that *being shorter than Wilt* is not an *intrinsic* property of the things that have it. In contrast, whether two people stand (in a certain order) in the *shorter-than* relation *does* depend only on their respective internal natures. The *shorter-than* relation is *intrinsic* in the sense that whether it holds between two people depends on nothing beyond the intrinsic natures of those people. (In just this way the notion of intrinsicalness is extended into the realm of all relations.)

I argued above that *ordinary thinghood* is not an intrinsic property, and urged that different ways of carving the world's stuff into things are available. This suggested that the property is *relational* – that there is a relation that it may be seen as projected from. Now I claim that this very *thing-for* relation is in fact intrinsic in the same way the *shorter-than* relation is, so that the property and relation of the example provide a solid analogy for the case at hand. Whether we (or Martians, etc.) view the stuff of a certain region as constituting a thing does not in fact depend on anything beyond the (intrinsic) way the stuff of that region is *and* the (intrinsic) way we (or they) are. So the *thing-for* relation is intrinsic. It is also true that the relation could be instantiated even in worlds without *us* whereas *ordinary thinghood* could not. (It is worth noting that there may be intrinsic properties that are coextensive with *ordinary thinghood* in the actual world. In fact it seems that there must be, given that the *thing-for* relation is intrinsic in the way I have claimed. Such intrinsic properties could of course be instantiated in worlds not containing us.) So the very features that seem to account for our intuition that *shorter than* is more fundamental than *shorter than Wilt* are present, though perhaps not as transparently, in the case of *thing for* and *ordinary thinghood*. (In general, any property that is the projection of an intrinsic relation relative to a fixed contingent parameter will prove to be less fundamental in the way suggested.)

W. V. Quine has claimed, in a commendably naturalistic spirit, that a physical object " . . . comprises simply the content, however heterogeneous, of some portion of space-time, however disconnected and gerrymandered."[1] Many people have reacted to such liberalism with shock and dismay. The idea that the mereological sum of a certain distant atom during August of 1954, together with the southwestern quarter of the U. S. Capitol dome on the first midnight of 1991 and the Taj Mahal on all the irrational points of time during its full career, should comprise a bona fide thing is somehow too much. But why? Is there anything at stake here?

I don't believe so. Let's call the above described putative thing '*T*'. The claim that there is no such thing as *T* has only two plausible interpretations. The first concerns how we (or most of us anyway) ordinarily view the world. It amounts to the claim that there

[1] Quine (1960), p. 171.

is no such thing as *T* recognized in our ordinary, everyday ontology. This is surely correct, but it is clearly not something that Quine (or anyone else) should deny. His recognition of things like *T* is unaffected. It consists, roughly, in the view that a description of the contents of the physical world may legitimately contain quantifiers ranging over a domain including the likes of *T*. The other interpretation in effect just denies this.

But how could quantifying over *T* be illegitimate? If the charge is to have any philosophical significance, it must be that it would be illegitimate because *no such thing as* T *really exists*. Since this isn't a claim about everyday ontology, it must be a claim about the nature of the spatiotemporal region and the stuff it contains. Let's assume there is no dispute over whether the region is a region or whether that region contains a certain distribution of stuff. Then the charge must be that there is some feature that the region or its contained stuff lacks, a shortcoming that prevents the region from actually containing a *thing*. Well, we have seen this view already. It is merely the view that *being a thing* is an intrinsic feature enjoyed by the stuff of some regions and not by the stuff of others. But if we have agreed, as urged above, that our own (everyday) conception of thinghood is *not* dictated solely by the intrinsic features of the stuff occupying various regions, but essentially involves *us* as well, then this idea seems quite incredible. To accept it would be to believe that there is nevertheless some independent, nonrelational property of *thinghood* with which our own admittedly relational one might or might not happen to agree extensionally. This is surely too much to believe. (Though, again, it is certainly true that *ordinary thinghood* is coextensive with various intrinsic properties of things. The point is that it is unreasonable to think of any of these properties as some absolute property of *being a thing*.)

So far I am in apparent accord with Hilary Putnam, who writes:

> [T]he same situation can be described in many different ways, depending on how we use the words. The situation does not itself legislate how words like "object," "entity," and "exist" must be used. What is wrong with the notion of objects existing "independently" of conceptual schemes is that there are no standards for the use of even the logical notions apart from conceptual choices.[2]

[2] Putnam (1988), p. 114. I should note that Putnam draws conclusions about "realism" from this observation that I would emphatically reject.

Putnam regards the question of how to divide the universe into objects as one calling for a *convention*. (See pp. 112–13.) Quine's naturalistic way would then be viewed as one of the available conventions – the *maximal* convention in the sense that it recognizes more substantial physical things than does any of its alternatives.

So far I have merely defended Quine's conception against the charge that it is somehow *wrong*. In Putnam's terms, this is just to argue that it is one of the available conventions. But I think there is more to be said for it than this, and I think there are hints of what more can be said in the argument for its legitimacy. For that argument shows there is no (logically consistent) way to be wrong. Conceptions that conflict with our everyday notions are, despite this inconvenience, above ontological reproach. If our goal is to describe the physical universe, and we seek a conception of "thing" to enlist in this effort, then Quine's maximal conception has much in its favor. For one thing, it is remarkably simple. The criterion for being a thing is, roughly, just occupying any spatiotemporal region, where regions may be thought of as corresponding one-to-one with sets of space-time points. Nothing could be simpler. And the maximality of this simple conception gives it the greatest possible theoretical flexibility. If some of the "reified" objects do us no good, we may ignore them. No harm done. And where they serve some useful purpose, we are better off having them than not. When there is no ontological price to pay, a maximal theory is the best bargain around.

But maybe Quine's convention isn't really maximal. It could be held that the very points of space-time, and the regions they comprise, are also physical things.[3] So, where a region is unoccupied, we could nevertheless speak of there being a thing if we took this step beyond Quine. And, in fact, even a fully occupied region would very naturally be held to be distinct from the thing that occupied it on this supermaximal view. (In a sense, that would give us two things "in" exactly the same region. Awkward, perhaps, but not absurd.) It seems to me that this is not a significant issue. Quine, after all, is *already* openly involved in quantification over regions of space-time. So any debate is merely over whether to view them as "physical objects." I think it violates intuition to do so. *Stuff* is the stuff of physical objects, and regions are not consti-

[3] Something like this may be Hartry Field's view. See Field (1980).

tuted by stuff (though they may of course contain stuff). So there is room to side with Quine and, in this last respect, with everyday opinion as well. We do not thereby give up regions, and, if we like, we may even regard them as *somehow* physical, though they will not be physical *objects* in the central sense. Quine's conception is maximal with respect to "stuffy" things even if one accepts regions as physical things. And if one does not, then it is just plain maximal.

So far I have tried to establish the ontological innocence of quantifying in this Quinean spirit over a domain including lots of strange mereological sums. From now on I will assume just such a maximal conception. But in the next chapter I will try to give it some further refinement and elaboration. In particular, I will deal with the question of how this conception meshes with ordinary views about persistence and change.

2. PROPERTIES

In the above discussion I have referred freely to various supposed properties and relations. I will continue to do this without offering any detailed justification. But I will make explicit a few assumptions about the nature of these supposed entities. First, I assume that properties, relations, and also propositions are "abstract" entities that exist independently of minds and languages. In saying they are abstract I mean they do not occupy any regions of space-time (and of course they are not identical with any regions of space-time). I think this is what people normally have in mind when they speak of "Platonism" about properties, relations, and propositions. So I will be openly Platonistic about these entities in this book. A number of more specific claims about properties and, especially, propositions will be made in Chapter 5. Apart from these, I don't think any of the main claims of this book depend crucially on the Platonism. Nominalist versions of the arguments could be given, but there are reasons for not trying to give them. One is that it would complicate matters to a distracting degree. Another is that the independence of the main conclusions from the Platonism should be pretty evident to the reader. (A third is that I actually accept the Platonism.)

So now we have properties. But how many? David Lewis has held that we have two different conceptions of properties: "sparse" and "abundant." He characterizes the sparse properties as those that account for genuine similarity, those of which " . . . there are only just enough . . . to characterise things completely and without redundancy." In contrast, the abundant properties go unimaginably further. They " . . . may be as extrinsic, as gruesomely gerrymandered, as miscellaneously disjunctive, as you please."[4] Mere "Cambridge" properties, like *singing in Vienna or made of ice*, are relatively innocent examples of abundance.

I don't think it is really true that our ordinary conceptual scheme includes two conceptions. I think it is more likely that each of us has a rather vague, single conception that lies somewhere between the sparse and the abundant, and that our conceptions vary pretty significantly among us. But they tend to rule out lots of Cambridge (and worse) properties, and rule in more properties than would be needed to do the work Lewis assigns to the sparse. This is because Lewis's sparse notion is really a "technical" one. Just what properties are needed to characterize things completely and without redundancy – assuming there is such a (unique) totality – is a technical question whose answer is certainly unknown. (Does it all boil down to a few properties of quarks, for example?) It would be very surprising to find that the answer to this question happened to be already present in our shared conceptual scheme.

Something like Lewis's dual conception is, I think, far more likely to be found among Platonist philosophers who feel a little uncomfortable about their Platonism. (The nonsparse "properties" are second-class citizens.) But no matter. If I am right, we have so far uncovered (at least) *three* different conceptions of properties: sparse, abundant, and intermediate. And since we find significant variations in the intermediate realm, we really have an indefinite number. This may begin to sound familiar. The question of what to count as a *property* is superficially analogous to the question of what to count as a *thing*: Different answers may at first seem equally defensible, and so it may seem a mere matter of convention. This impression is enhanced by the fact that lots of putative properties are certainly "redundant" in the presence of others. This, of course, partly underlies any impulse in favor of sparseness. But what is important is that it reinforces the feeling of conventionality, and so the sense of analogy with the case of things.

[4] Lewis (1986), pp. 59–60.

But the analogy is strained. Our fundamental ontological position is that there is lots of stuff spread here and there and now and then throughout space-time. It does seem a matter of convention which "parcels" of such stuff are to count as *things*. The "thing-structure" of the distribution of stuff is something *we* impose in one way or another for various possible purposes. *This* is the stuff of convention. But we have opted for full-strength Platonism about properties. This means their existence is independent of our conceptual schemes and various purposes. Hence, to favor, say, Lewis's sparse properties, would *not* be to adopt a convention, but rather to take a real stand on what there is and isn't. It might be that the evidence supporting the original postulation of properties could be mined to support one or another such stand.

I believe that evidence for properties in fact favors an abundant realm, and I will assume abundance throughout this book.[5] The reason is roughly as follows. Properties are the sorts of entities that get expressed by predicates of our language. (Note that this is not to argue for the existence of properties from "linguistic data." Far from it. It's just a fact about the relation of properties – if they exist – to our language.) Now, are there reasons to think that some predicates express properties but others don't? Well, there is at least one very good reason: the threat of paradox. (Consider the predicate 'is a non–self-instantiating property'.) But are there any good reasons for thinking that a predicate that may *without paradox* be assumed to express a property nevertheless does not express a property? I think the answer is no. Everyday intuitions that certain predicates don't express properties are, I believe, manifestations of our local interests and conceptual scheme, and should not be considered to have serious ontological import.

Without going into details, a couple of points may help motivate this. Often what drives such intuitions is a combination of redundancy and either infrequency of instantiation or comparative uselessness given our constitution and interests. We don't recognize such properties because we just don't have much use for them. And often, I think, these intuitions reflect our refusal to count certain sorts of regionalized stuff as constituting *things*. Predicates that

[5] More on abundance, including a theory of abundant properties, may be found in Jubien (1989*a*). For a somewhat different but more elaborately developed position, see Bealer (1982).

could never apply to officially acknowledged things, but do apply to officially unreified regionalized stuff, tend not to be seen as expressing properties. (This also exposes an unfortunate tendency to think of properties as applying only to things, as may be seen in Lewis's characterization of the sparse properties. But of course we unhesitatingly attribute properties to mere stuff on a daily basis.) I believe that either different patterns of usefulness or a different conception of thing would result in our everyday recognition of a different array of properties. All of this makes it seem too parochial to put much ontological weight on our everyday opinions. It seems much more satisfactory to think that a fully abundant realm of properties is really there, but that for various local reasons we don't need to worry about most of them. For better or worse, this will be the view in what follows.

3. POSSIBLE WORLDS

I am skeptical about the existence of possible worlds. This skepticism extends to every general sort of possible world that has to my knowledge been proposed. Notably, it extends to Lewis-style "concrete" worlds, and to all manner of "abstract" worlds, including "linguistic" worlds,[6] worlds based on propositions (or "states of affairs"),[7] and worlds taken as primitive entities of their own distinctive sort or as primitive, "functional" notions.[8] My suspicions about worlds have been given in detail elsewhere,[9] and I won't try to repeat them in this book. Nor will I say why I don't think we need worlds anyway, but I don't.

Despite this, I think possible worlds are extremely useful as a metaphor in discussing modality. They give a special vividness to our imaginings about what is possible. More importantly, they help us think clearly about complicated questions of modal *truth* because they may be mapped to the indices (or so-called possible worlds) of various formal systems of semantics for modal logic (and modalized theories generally). This makes them invaluable in detailed modal analysis. But neither of these uses requires any real

[6] See, for example, Adams (1974).
[7] See, for example, Plantinga (1974), especially Chapter 4.
[8] See Stalnaker (1984), Chapter 3. [9] See Jubien (1988).

ontological commitment to worlds. We may still view them as mere metaphor. So that will be my position here. I will make free metaphorical use of worlds while carefully avoiding ontological commitments of any of the sorts that typical world theorists have made.

2

Things and their parts

1. INTRODUCTION

Our next task is to sharpen the maximal, naturalistic, Quinean notion of *thing* discussed in Chapter 1. The first step will be to introduce a simple theory treating *substantial physical things*. This theory will later provide a basis for the discussion of the topics of ordinary proper names and necessity. The theory to be presented is in some ways idealized. Its maximality, for example, might be seen as an idealization, but we have already seen the reasons that favor it. More important is the theory's likely departure from "ultimate physical truth" – likely, at least, if contemporary physics is correct in certain of its main doctrines.

Let me mention two areas where the theory may conflict with physics. First, it takes as primitive the idea of a point of space-time being "occupied." Each point of space-time either definitely is or definitely is not occupied – it isn't a matter of probability distributions or the like. This may be impossible to reconcile with quantum theory. Second, it may be just as hard to reconcile with relativity theory. Nothing in the theory is relativized to inertial frames. It simply assumes a fixed, four-dimensional coordinatization of space-time, in the sense of an association of ordered quadruples of real numbers with individual points of space-time, which may be thought of simply as an association of names with things named. (Nothing is assumed about the geometry or metric of space-time.) But treating the occupancy of points as absolute may conflict with the relativistic denial of absolute simultaneity.

These apparent conflicts would be very suspicious if the theory were to be put to various conceivable uses. But I think our use of it will prove to be above suspicion. We need to talk carefully about certain aspects of things *in a general way*, so having a *theory* will be a great help. The aspects in question include the apparent fact that things can get *named* and *referred to*, and the fact that they may have certain properties as a matter of *necessity*. For *most* purposes like these, the question of whether a particular thing has an absolutely definite temporal beginning, or whether instead we must say it has a range of beginnings (or whatever) corresponding to various inertial frames, may safely be set aside. Likewise, the question of whether the thing occupies a completely definite region right now, or whether it instead only occupies it with a certain probability (and occupies various other regions with other probabilities), may safely be set aside.

It is, of course, possible to raise certain questions within our domain of concern whose answers may depend on the ultimate physical facts. An example might be whether a thing has a certain precise temporal career *of necessity*. Whether the denial of absolute simultaneity really does affect this is certainly worthy of discussion – the answer isn't obvious. When we touch on such questions in what follows, any conclusions should be regarded as appropriately hedged. For questions like whether a thing is necessarily made of wood, the ultimate physical niceties are irrelevant, so we may consider these questions against the background of the idealized theory without this sort of worry.

Of course I will assume that physics is consistent with the existence of things that we ordinarily think we can name and refer to, like tables and chairs. (So much the worse for physics if it isn't.) In one guise or another, these entities had better be found among the objects that physics tolerates. In other words, they should be found among the objects that any plausible and complete *ontology*, consistent with physics, accepts. The central philosophical concern in this book is with just these entities. It is only for the sake of *simplicity* that we are going to pretend that they definitely occupy exquisitely definite regions of space-time, and for the sake of *generality* that we will parlay this pretense into an overall theory of things. It is important to note that we do not want to assume, *even from the standpoint of the theory*, that the question of precisely when a certain table begins to exist, or precisely what space it takes up, is beyond dispute. But a dispute would mean that there are slightly different things that are plausible candidates for being the table. (I'm not sure that the question of which one "really is" the table actually makes good sense.) The pretense of the theory is *not* that some specific one of the candidates is *definitely* the table. It is merely that each one of the *candidates* has a definite beginning and occupies a definite location.

The subject matter of the theory has been restricted to "substantial physical things." I believe the ultimate conclusions about names and necessity also hold for other sorts of things, but developing them would require a more general background, and that would introduce unwanted complications. The virtues of avoiding nonphysical things are evident enough, but a word about the restriction to *substantial* things is certainly in order.

The main point of the restriction is to avoid the possibility of having more than one (physical) object precisely and entirely in one and the same spatiotemporal region. Thus we must avoid things like localized *fields*, which might very well preside in precisely the region occupied by some more substantial physical object. Intuitively, fields do not *occupy* regions in the first place – they are merely *affections* of regions. So fields, under this intuitive account, are not substantial. The theory will accept this intuition and ignore the fields.

But here is an objection. What if it turns out to be a consequence of ultimate physics that there really is nothing but space-time, and even everyday things like tables are just local fields of certain sorts? Wouldn't that make the theory vacuous? The answer is no. It would, however, mean that the theory should be reconstrued as treating *certain* fields (or combinations of fields, etc.) to the exclusion of others. Fields of certain specifiable sorts would be regarded as "things" (or "objects," etc.), the others would not. The point is that our theoretical interest here is simply to honor a certain difference, regardless of its underlying basis. But even without fields (or without fields of the "insubstantial" kind), there remains room to think that more than one thing *can* occupy exactly the same region. Perhaps a statue and a (reified) quantity of clay. This is a question we will consider later.

2. THE THEORY **M**

The theory **M** is extremely simple. It has just one primitive notion and just one axiom. Later we will extend it by adding a further axiom. Here is an informal presentation of **M**.

First we assume a fixed, four-dimensional coordinatization of space-time. Our primitive is the notion of a point of space-time being *occupied*. Now we give two definitions: (*i*) A *region* (*of space-time*) is any nonempty set of points of space-time. (*ii*) A region is *full* iff all of its points are occupied. Now for the single axiom: If a region is full, then exactly one thing occupies all of its points and no others. That's the whole theory.

So **M** really is a very simple theory. Still, it is worth being explicit about certain of its features. To begin, it might be slightly more satisfactory from an ontological perspective if *regions* were taken not as *sets* of points of space-time, but rather as the actual *portions* of space-time that are constituted by those points. But it is technically a little smoother if the official definition makes them sets. So let us leave it this way, but informally regard the term as systematically ambiguous between the two senses. (Context always makes it clear which sense is the more suitable.)

An immediate consequence of the axiom is that a region composed of exactly one point of space-time is occupied by exactly one thing that occupies no other points. So **M** makes room for some very small things, to put it mildly. (Equally mildly, these things are also very brief.) A thing that occupies only one point may be called a *point-object* or *point-whole*. Given that any regions are occupied at all – something that is true but, quite properly, isn't asserted by the theory – there must be some point-objects. Point-objects are of course not recognized in everyday ontology. They are the first symptom of the maximality of **M**.

It is important to get used to the idea that (a region constituted by) a point may be occupied by many things. It is occupied by only one point-whole, but, intuitively, that point-whole is a part of an indefinite number of more-extensive things (given that there is lots of physical stuff). And each of these more–extensive things may properly be said to occupy that point. So if *p* is some point occupied by a point-whole that is part of my toe, it follows that my toe, my foot, and I all occupy *p*. And so does the world's population, if we construe it as the "scattered object" consisting of everyone's bodies.

Scattered objects are of course further manifestations of the maximality of **M**. It is important to notice that objects may be scattered only spatially, only temporally, or in both ways at once. Most scattered objects are not recognized in our ordinary ontology, but it is very clear that some are. Libraries, in the sense of the physical books, are scattered, and so are bicycles when they are disassembled. (We do not believe that a bicycle goes out of existence when taken apart, only to pop back into existence upon reassembly. Instead we say the bicycle is disassembled.) Scattered objects are of course among the most notorious examples of what are often called *mereological sums*. From now on I will use the terms 'thing' and 'object' to mean *substantial physical thing* in the sense of the theory **M.** Sometimes, to emphasize maximality, I will use the term 'mereological sum'.

Here are some further definitions and elaborations. (*iii*) If a thing occupies all and only the points of some region (as every thing must) then we also say that the region *absorbs* the thing. (Note that, in this usage, a more-inclusive region does *not* absorb the thing.) We are now in a position to define a "part–whole" relation that has the key properties that are associated with the part–whole relation of classical mereology (or the calculus of individuals).[1] (*iv*) If x and y are any things, then x is *part of* y iff the region that absorbs x is a subset of the region that absorbs y. (It should be clear that, in this sense, a 'part' is much more like an *arbitrary portion* than, say, a *detachable component*.) So defined, the *part-of* relation is transitive and reflexive, so it conforms to the standard notion from mereology. (Of course it is an easy matter to define an irreflexive *proper-part-of* relation.) (*v*) If x is a thing that exists at least at the instant t, then the t-*slice* of x is the most inclusive part of x that exists only at t. To say that a thing exists "at t" is, officially, to say that the region that absorbs it contains at least one point whose time-coordinate is t. (*vi*) If x is the t-slice of y, then any part of x (including x itself) may be called a t-part of y. The t-parts of a thing of course exist only at t. (*vii*) A thing is called a t-*object* iff it exists only at t. Thus t-slices and t-parts of things are t-objects in their own right. (We may also call a t-object *instantaneous* because it exists only at the instant t.)

3. A FORMAL VERSION OF M

It is not difficult to see from the informal presentation that **M** may be stated as a formal first-order theory. In this brief section we pro-

[1] For an illuminating discussion and further references, see Goodman (1951), especially Section 2.4.

vide explicit first-order versions of the axiom, a corollary, and the definitions. We use 'Oxp' to mean that the thing x occupies the space-time point p. We use 'x', 'y', and 'z' as variables over things, 'p' and 'q' over points, 'r' and 's' over regions (in the sense of sets of points), and 't' over times.

Definitions:

(*i*) A *region* (*of space-time*) is any nonempty set of points of space-time.

(*ii*) A region r is *full* ('Fr') iff $\forall p(p \in r \supset \exists x Oxp)$.

Axiom (The Principle of Wholes):

$$Fr \supset \exists! x \forall p (Oxp \equiv p \in r).$$

Corollary (The Principle of Point-wholes):

$$\exists x Oxp \supset \exists! x(Oxp \;\&\; \forall q(Oxq \supset q = p)).$$

Definitions:

(*iii*) r *absorbs* x ('Arx') iff

$$\forall p(Oxp \equiv p \in r).$$

(*iv*) x is *part of* y ('Pxy') iff

$$\exists r \exists s (Arx \;\&\; Asy \;\&\; r \subseteq s).$$

(*v.i*) The *time-coordinate of* p ('$tc(p)$') is readily definable in first-order set theory given any conventional reduction of ordered quadruples to sets.

(*v.ii*) r is a t-*region* ('Rtr') iff

$$\forall p(p \in r \supset tc(p) = t).$$

(*v.iii*) A t-region r is the t-*slice of* a region s ('$Strs$') iff $r \subseteq s$ &

$$\exists p(p \in s \;\&\; tc(p) = t) \;\&\; \forall p[(p \in s \;\&\; tc(p) = t) \supset p \in r].$$

(*v.iv*) x is the t-*slice of* y ('$Stxy$') iff

$$Pxy \;\&\; \forall r \forall s[(Arx \;\&\; Asy) \supset Strs].$$

(*vi*) x is a t-*part of* y ('$Ptxy$') iff

$$Pxy \;\&\; \exists r(Rtr \;\&\; Arx).$$

(*vii*) x is a t-*object* iff $\exists r(Rtr \;\&\; Arx)$.

4. THE THEORY **M+**

In this section we extend **M** to a *modal* first-order theory by adding a modal axiom. The axiom is the much-maligned principle of mereological essentialism. This principle holds that things have their parts essentially. A slightly more explicit statement is this: If

x is a part of y, then it is necessary that if y exists, then x exists and is part of y. Using the formula '$\exists w(w = y)$' (and variants) to express *y exists,* we may state the principle formally as follows:

$$\forall x \forall y[Pxy \supset \Box (\exists w(w = y) \supset \exists z(z = x \,\&\, Pxy))].$$

The theory **M+** is obtained from **M** by adding this statement as a new axiom.

The principle of mereological essentialism is not refuted by examples of things changing their parts over time. This is because it says nothing about whether things can change their parts over time. This, in turn, is because it says nothing about *time* – it's a purely *modal* principle. Suppose that a thing x has part y at t. If a mereological essentialist holds that any part of a thing has a *temporal* aspect, then he is free to allow that y need not be a part of x at any time other than t, though he is of course committed to the view that y is necessarily a part of x at t. We will have much to say about this matter later, and will see that not only are essentialists of this sort *free* to hold that y isn't a part of x at times other than t, they are actually committed to it. But let us set time aside for the moment. Many have thought the principle must be false because it conflicts with clear and distinct *modal* intuitions. Here is an example of such an intuition.

Suppose you are building a house and the job is just about complete. What remains is to nail on one more shingle. Two relevantly similar loose shingles remain. You pick shingle A and nail it on. You set shingle B aside for a doghouse you're planning to build. All will agree that you could have picked shingle B and set shingle A aside instead. If you had, you would still have the same house, but it would have a somewhat different inventory of parts. It is concluded that shingle A is not necessarily a part of your house. But this means that at least one part of your house is not necessarily a part of your house. This is held to be enough to refute the principle.

I don't think it does. To see why, I want us briefly to forget the example and think about things in the abstract, in isolation from everyday descriptions and associations. So first recall that an arbitrary thing is just the occupier of some arbitrary, full region of space-time. Let x be any such arbitrary thing, and let y be an arbitrary proper part of x. Now, by the principle of wholes, there also exists a third thing – the thing that is all of x except for the part

y. Let's call it z. If we agree to use '+' and '−' in the natural way for mereological sum and difference, we have $z = x - y$. Now imagine another situation, as much like this situation as possible, but in which the entire thing y simply does not exist. This certainly *seems* like a situation in which x doesn't exist either, but z does. I think it is very difficult to deny this intuition without somehow relying on prior convictions involving everyday descriptions and associations, like the belief that a certain *house* could have had (somewhat) different parts.

Now back to the example. I think the key intuitions in the examples are actually correct, but I still don't think it refutes the principle. In order to refute the principle, the example must provide some *thing* that has a part that *it* might not have had. But does it? Well, several things play roles in the example. Two of them already have names, the shingles A and B. Let's use 'U' to name the large, houselike entity that does not include A (or B). Then two other important things in the story are the mereological sums $U + A$ and $U + B$. For simplicity let's pretend that $U + A$ is *always* the house, even when it's a scattered object. This means that U is *never* the house, even though for part of the story it's an "unfinished house." Other interpretive options exist, but the differences don't really bear on the present discussion. So $U + A$ is the house and $U + B$ isn't, but the key point of the story is that it could have been the other way around. Now A is the part that some thing is supposed to have only contingently. But again, what thing? Well, it can't be either U or $U + B$ since neither has A as a part in the first place.

Perhaps it is $U + A$. After all, $U + A$ is the house! But it can't be $U + A$ either, for $U + A$ would still exist and have A as a part if the house had been completed using shingle B, and A had been reserved for the doghouse. In my opinion there are no other significant candidates.

Against this it may be held that I haven't listed all the things the example provides: Somehow I haven't listed "the house." I was wrong to claim that $U + A$ was the house (and I would have been just as wrong if I had chosen any of the other available mereological sums). I was misled by the accidental fact that the house and $U + A$ happen to occupy precisely the same spatiotemporal region! (If shingle B had been used, then the house would have occupied exactly the region occupied by $U + B$.) Well, there are two interestingly different ways to elaborate this nonnaturalistic sort of reply. In a strictly neutral spirit, let's call them the *mysterious* and the *mystical*.

The mysterious view is inconsistent with **M+**. It holds that the house is just another humdrum physical object, with no notable features setting it apart from any other physical object. It just happens to occupy exactly the same region as $U + A$ and, moreover, it just happens to be made of exactly the same stuff as $U + A$! Whereas, in general, the stuff occupying a given fully occupied region just constitutes one physical thing, here we have a case where it constitutes two. I think the mysterious view is just too mysterious to be believed as long as there is a plausible account that reconciles intuitions like the ones that drive the example with a "nonproliferative" theory of objects (like **M+**). I will offer such an account below.

The mystical view *is* consistent with **M+**. According to this view, the house isn't a purely physical object. It has $U + A$ as a physical part, but it also has a nonphysical part or aspect. It is the nonphysical element that gives it its "identity." If this nonphysical element were to be "joined" to some other suitable physical object, like $U + B$, then one and the same house would have different physical parts. We may think of the mystical view as a kind of dualism. Houses have "souls." The soul that a given house has is had by that house of necessity. The body that a given house has isn't. I don't think this is a plausible view of the nature of houses, but I'm not going to argue against it here. The reason is that it's consistent with **M+**. It *doesn't* undermine the mereological essentialism of **M+**, which is strictly a doctrine about physical objects. It may be incompatible with some more general version of mereological essentialism, in which sums of physical and nonphysical entities are admitted, but we have no commitment to such a doctrine here.

I want to conclude this section by sketching the view that I claim reconciles our intuitions about the example with the principle of mereological essentialism. Much more will be said about this view in what follows, but it will be useful to give the general thrust of it now. I think an important fallacy underlies the tendency to think the example refutes the principle. Let's do a quick review. What is at stake here is the validity of a certain argument. In prose, it goes something like this:

(1) A is a part of the house, but is not necessarily a part of the house.
Therefore:

(2) There is a thing of which A is a part but is not necessarily a part.

I agree that if (2) follows validly from (1), then the intuitions of the example, captured in (1), are enough to refute mereological essentialism. But I don't think the argument is valid. (2) may be formalized by:

(2*) $\exists x(PAx \ \& \ \neg\Box PAx)$.

Now, (2*)would follow nicely by existential generalization from:

(1*) $PAH \ \& \ \neg\Box PAH$.

And of course (1*) would be the natural first-order translation of (1) if the phrase 'the house' were a proper name. But it isn't. It looks more like a definite description (or an abbreviation of a definite description, like 'the house we are considering').[2] Here is the normal Russellian formalization of (1) under this assumption:

(1**) $\exists x(Hx \ \& \ \forall y(Hy \supset y = x) \ \& \ PAx \ \& \ \neg\Box PAx)$.

This formulation definitely entails (2*). Under our assumption, it has the same meaning as the (awkward) English sentence:

(1′) Some thing is the house and has A as a part, but does not necessarily have A as a part.

Now, I think (1′) is false. So, since I think (1) is true, I think (1**) is a bad translation of (1). I claim (1′) [and (1**)] is false because it seems to me that the thing that is the house and has A as a part is our old friend $U + A$, and $U + A$ necessarily has A as a part. This, of course, would merely be to beg the question in the absence of a plausible explanation of the truth of (1).

So here is how I explain the truth of (1). I think there is a thing (in fact, $U + A$) that *is the house*. But I also think it is possible that some *other* thing *be the house*, a thing that does not have A as a part. (In fact, the example shows that $U + B$ is a thing that could have *been the house*, and $U + B$ doesn't have A as a part.) When we say the house (or any other familiar thing) could have had different parts, I think the most coherent metaphysical construal of our

[2] Examples with names will be discussed later.

claim is that some other *thing* could have *been the house*. And of course, under mereological essentialism, any *other* thing must have (some) different parts.

A likely and natural reaction is that this commits me to the often-ridiculed view that certain identity sentences express only contingent truths. For example, the sentence '$U + A$ is the house'. Since I think $U + B$ could have been the house, and, in any possible situation in which it is the house, it *isn't* $U + A$, it must be that the original identity is contingent.

But I don't think this is right. It isn't right because the 'is' in '$U + A$ is the house' isn't the *'is' of identity* in the first place! The proposition that sentence expresses is indeed contingent, but it's a contingent *predication*. It says that the thing $U + A$ has a certain property, the property of *being the house*. But this property is not an "identity property," that is, it isn't the (relational) property of being identical with some specific thing. What the example really shows is that a *different* thing ($U + B$) could have had this very *same* property. And, of course, A is not a part of $U + B$. So *some* thing could have *been the house* without having A as a part. *This*, I claim, is what lies behind the idiomatic but extremely misleading sentence, 'The house might not have had A as a part'. Using 'Hx' to mean *x is the house*, we may translate it as follows:

$$\exists x(Hx \;\&\; PAx \neg\Box\forall y(Hy \supset PAy)).$$

I will urge that there is abroad in the land a nearly universal tendency to take lots of "isses" of predication to be "isses" of identity. This tendency is fostered in many of the classic writings of modern philosophy, and it has gone virtually unnoticed and unchallenged – perhaps because it is often harmless. But it has caused a good bit of trouble in metaphysics, and I hope to undo some of the trouble in this book.

This tendency is really just a symptom of a deeper disorder in our normal philosophical thinking. That disorder is the belief that ordinary proper names and at least some definite descriptions actually *refer to* (or *denote*, or *designate*) specific entities. One of the central contentions of this book is that this belief is false, and that a myriad of major philosophical errors flow directly from it. I will call this belief the *Fallacy of Reference*.

Let me say a little more carefully just what it is that I am calling the Fallacy of Reference. Consider first a (specific token of a) sentence like 'Bill Clinton is a Democrat'. It expresses a certain proposition. Many people think the proposition it expresses is one in which a certain property (*being a Democrat*) is attributed to a certain specific entity (the "referent" of the name 'Bill Clinton'). In other words, many people think the sentence expresses a proposition that has a specific entity as a "constituent." Such people commit the Fallacy of Reference. Of course they do so without believing that what they are doing is in any way fallacious. Many people are perfectly content with the idea that some thing is the referent of 'Bill Clinton' and is a constituent of the proposition our sentence expresses. I hope to convince them that they are wrong.

Now consider the sentence 'The president is a Democrat'. Some people, though not all of the ones just discussed, also think that (a token of) this sentence expresses a proposition that has a specific entity (the "referent" of 'The president') as a constituent – that it attributes a certain property to a certain specific entity. In doing so they also commit the Fallacy of Reference. Most would deny that descriptions generally contribute specific constituents in this way, but would hold that certain descriptions do, or that certain descriptions do under certain circumstances. For example, it could be argued that the description in (1) does, on the grounds that the utterer of (1) is surely saying something that goes well beyond the fact that we might have been considering an entirely different house (or that an entirely different house might have been built on the site in question, etc.). This point is surely right, but we will see that it isn't enough to show that the description contributes a specific constituent to the proposition the sentence expresses. That conclusion follows only if we commit the Fallacy of Reference.

So, by the Fallacy of Reference I mean the belief that proper names or (certain) definite descriptions *refer* in the specific sense described in the cases just discussed. (The terms 'denote' and 'designate' will hereafter be used synonymously with 'refer' in this sense.) Notice that the fallacy readily accounts for the above inference of (2) from (1), as follows. We commit the fallacy by taking the description 'the house' to refer to a certain specific thing. But then, since (1) informs us that "the house" has a certain property, it follows immediately that there is a certain specific thing that has that very same property. In other words, (2) follows validly from (1) in the presence of the fallacy. But alas, I reject the fallacy, so I may happily reject (2) and accept the principle of mereological essentialism. I will do just this and will hence adopt **M+** as the official theory of things. I believe this strategy has now been shown to be logically coherent. Whether it is ultimately reasonable will depend, among other things, on a plausible account of such supposed properties as *being this house* and *being Bill Clinton*.

5. PERSISTENCE VERSUS TEMPORAL PARTS

I recently heard a commercial on the radio for a company that leases cars. Part of it went something like this:

Salesman: And, ah, Mr. Smith, just how much of the car did you want to have?
Customer: Uh, I was thinking in terms of the whole thing.
Salesman: I see. So you plan on having it for . . . well, for quite a long time . . . ?
Customer: Not really. Maybe three, four years.
Salesman: Ah, then you don't want the whole thing after all, you only want three or four years of it! But then why buy the whole thing in the first place? Why not just buy the part you want?!

Are the things of our everyday acquaintance *three*-dimensional objects that "persist through time," or are they *four*-dimensional objects that have "temporal parts"? I think the commercial illustrates two things. First, that our everyday conception is the former and, second, that the latter is not so alien that it cannot be made to appeal to common sense. The issue of persistence versus temporal parts has been widely discussed in the literature.[3] I will not try to give a thorough survey of what has been said. Instead I will make what I think is the best case for temporal parts in the present section. In the following two sections I will turn first to an important issue concerning temporal parts and, second, to a significant argument against them.

I have already conceded that our ordinary, everyday conception of things is that they are three-dimensional entities that persist through time. To adopt a temporal-parts account is therefore to depart from common sense on just this point. This is a definite disadvantage, but one that I think is outweighed by the dramatic disadvantages of sticking with common sense. I will now try to

[3] Some considerations against temporal parts are presented in Geach (1967–8), Chisholm (1973), Thomson (1983), and van Inwagen (1990*a*) and (1990*b*).

motivate this claim. The following discussion is meant to be taken in the language of well-informed common sense, independent of theories of names and the like.

Suppose that on Monday you visit a furniture store and see a table that you like. Let's call it 'T'. You write a check and the salesman promises to have it delivered to your home the next day. On Tuesday a truck pulls up and a table is brought into your house. Let's call the table now in your house 'T^*'. But during the unloading a small chip was knocked off the inside of one of the legs, coming to rest on the floor of the truck. Let's call this chip 'C'. When you inspect the table you notice that it's been chipped, but you see that the chipped area is very small and inconspicuous. You decide you can live with it and you make no complaint. In reflecting on the matter, in your commonsensical way, you reach the following two conclusions. First, you are satisfied that your new table is the one you saw in the store yesterday. Second, you think that somewhere, unless it was destroyed, there is a small wooden object that was once part of the table, but is no longer. None of this disturbs you.

But it disturbs me. I think it means that some object, T, fully present on a certain occasion, has a property that some object, T^*, fully present on a different occasion, *lacks*. The property is: *having* C *as a part*. I think that if T has a property that T^* lacks, then T cannot be identical with T^*. I think this even if the property in question is a relational one, like *having* C *as a part*.

I am not sure whether the principle of the indiscernibility of identicals is rightly regarded as commonsensical. I do think it's entirely *obvious* once one becomes clear about just what it says, but sometimes it seems to take a bit more than common sense to arrive at the needed clarity. At any rate, I would say this: If the principle does belong to common sense, then common sense is apparently contradictory in holding the persistence doctrine along with it. And if it isn't part of common sense, it is nevertheless so clearly true that the conflict should be resolved by abandoning persistence.

On the doctrine of temporal parts, for example as codified in **M+**, it is simply false that T is identical with T^*. T and T^* occupy different regions of space-time, so they are automatically distinct things. If our ontology is that of **M+**, then we will say this. There is a table, say τ. Both T and T^* are parts of τ. Neither T nor T^* is a table. They are notable in being the spatially maximal parts of τ

that exist at the times at which they exist. The common sense intuition that T is "the same table as" T^* is to be explained merely by noting that they are spatially maximal temporal parts of a single table. That table is of course identical with itself. And T is also identical with itself; same for T^*. But, to repeat, T is not identical with T^*. They stand to each other in the important relation of being distinct, spatially maximal temporal parts of one and the same table. This is not the identity relation, but it is the relation that common sense may have mistaken for the identity relation in the case of the table.

Persistence theories inevitably have to explain so-called identity over time. They have to explain how it is that T (on Monday) can be *identical* with T^* (on Tuesday), when all agree that T and T^* have different properties. This is a difficult order to fill because the problem has been created *by the theory itself*, and it's nevertheless a problem about *identity*. The results are always disappointing, involving complex "identity conditions," wholesale time-relativization of properties, treating instantiation as a ternary relation, or other highly problematic metaphysical maneuvers.

Temporal-parts theories encounter no such problems. The notion of identity is absolute, necessary, and also wholly trivial. Everything is identical with itself, as a matter of necessity. Nothing is identical with anything other than itself, as a matter of necessity. The very idea of identity over time is absurd (unless it merely means that temporally extended things are identical with themselves). To say that a thing existing at one time is identical with a thing existing at another time is either false or else it is best construed as meaning that the two things are parts of some significant further thing. Now of course it may be difficult to *decide* whether the two things are parts of a single table. Or it may be difficult to say *in general* what it would take for two things to be parts of a single table. But the former is merely an epistemic problem, and the latter is *not* a problem about *identity*. It's a problem about the concept of *tablehood*. (What differences of properties can the different temporal parts of a thing display if that thing is a *table*?)

Thus I believe the major disadvantage of persistence accounts is that they *create* difficult metaphysical problems – problems about identity that have no evident solutions. The major disadvantage for temporal-parts accounts is that they force us to acknowledge that some of the things we ordinarily say are literally false. But this just means we must provide a charitable reconstrual of some of our ordinary talk.

6. THE BOUNDARIES OF THINGS

The entities ranged over by the quantifiers of **M+**, however extensive or nonextensive (!) they may be, all occupy absolutely specific regions of space-time. This raises an interesting modal question: Suppose *x* occupies precisely the (full) region *R*. Might *x* have occupied some region other than *R*? **M+** is compatible with different answers. Mark Heller, a staunch proponent of temporal parts, favors a negative answer:

> A given four-dimensional object goes out of existence at the time that it does because the object's boundaries are its defining characteristics. The material content of either a temporally larger or temporally smaller region of spacetime is, by definition, a different four-dimensional hunk of matter. It is because of the nature of a four-dimensional object that it has just those spatiotemporal boundaries and no others . . . a four-dimensional hunk of matter, by its very nature, has its spatiotemporal boundaries essentially.[4]

Heller's overall position is too involved to present in full detail, but it is a compelling position. I will soon adopt an opposing view, but first I will try to say briefly why Heller holds his. According to Heller, we often act *as if* there are certain objects even though such objects may not really exist. When speaking as if they existed, Heller calls them "conventional objects." What makes for a conventional object is the fact that "we have certain conventions that lead us to act as if there is an object that has [such and such] persistence conditions and essential properties" – conditions and properties that are *independent* of the physical structures of the purported objects (pp. 39*ff*). It is, to put it in a very rough way, a matter of our (normally unwittingly) adopting the *convention* that there exist objects with such and such modal properties. But it is the *non*-conventional objects that really exist. In the example of the previous section, Heller would likely say that *the house* is a conventional object, while the various mereological sums are nonconventional.[5]

[4] Heller (1990), p. 53.
[5] See Chapter 2, especially Section 6.

Nonconventional objects, which Heller calls "four-dimensional hunks of matter," are very much like the objects treated by the theory **M+**. (But there is no invariable parallel to conventional objects. Sometimes they are objects of **M+**, sometimes they don't exist at all.) **M+**, of course, is silent on the major question before us. It says only that things occupy specific, precise regions, and they have their parts essentially. It doesn't say whether or not they could have had different spatiotemporal locations. So Heller's nonconventional objects might as well be thought of as objects of **M+**, and we may see him as extending the theory by adding the further claim that the exact region a thing fills is the only region it could have filled. I am going to dissent in the following qualified way. I will claim that the objects of **M+** are best thought of as having their *spatial* locations accidentally, but as having their *temporal* locations essentially. I believe the disagreement here is strictly over which of several conventions is to be preferred. Hence I will be claiming that my choice fits best with our normal intuitions and in particular does so better than Heller's. (The extent to which Heller would view the dispute as concerning a convention is not clear to me.)

Now why does Heller think objects have their spatiotemporal boundaries essentially? He thinks they do because to hold otherwise would be, in effect, to transform them into conventional objects. He gives the following argument:

> Notice . . . that if an object could have had a spatiotemporal position other than the one that it in fact has, then two objects with matching material configurations could have had each other's locations . . . [But in such a case we would] seem to have two possible worlds with exactly the same material configuration.
>
> But identity cannot be so independent of material configuration. There cannot be two worlds that are exactly alike except for the identities of the objects that exist at those worlds, unless those supposed identities are conventional. (p. 56)

I don't agree that the world in which the locations of the things are switched is a world with exactly the same "material configuration" as the original world, so I think the argument fails. I don't agree because I think the *stuff* of the two worlds is differently distributed, something that may be said quite independently of the matter of conventional versus nonconventional *objects*. So I think the worlds do not differ *only* in the identities of the objects (in certain locations), since this difference in the identities of objects itself depends on a further difference – a difference in the distribution of stuff.

It is certainly true that the worlds may in some reasonable sense be "qualitatively indiscernible." But I think that's irrelevant. If easily discriminable things could have had each other's location, then surely so could things with "matching material configurations," if this merely meant qualitatively indiscernible things. And I will argue below that easily discriminable things indeed could have had each other's locations. But, to think this is not, in and of itself, to make the things conventional in Heller's sense. For it doesn't make their modal properties independent of their material configurations in any reasonable sense of that term. It doesn't do this because the possibility of switched locations for the things merely reflects possibilities for the stuff that constitutes those things. But that stuff certainly ought to count as part of the "material configuration" of the things it constitutes. It is somewhat puzzling that Heller does not accept this himself, for he is perfectly willing to speak of matter as "filling up regions of spacetime" and to say that a "physical object is the material content of a region of spacetime" (p. 4).

But why do I think easily discriminable things could have had each other's locations in the first place? Let us begin with two things Heller might view as conventional: a plain gold sphere and a plain silver sphere of the same size. Surely it is possible for the state of affairs that we would *ordinarily* describe as their (rough) locations having been switched at an earlier time to have occurred. Then the gold one would have been about where the silver one actually is. And surely this might have been done in such a way that some proper part – perhaps very small – of the one would at this very instant fully occupy *precisely* the region in fact fully occupied by a proper part of the other. Now, from the point of view of **M+** (and Heller), these instantaneous proper parts are legitimate things. They are the occupiers of certain regions of space-time, and the point is that the switching of the spheres would have resulted in these proper parts having occupied different regions, in fact each other's. But these proper parts are also *non*conventional, even if the spheres of which they are parts are not. Furthermore, they are easily discriminable, since they are parts of easily discriminable, easily perceptible, nonoverlapping objects.

Of course the ultimate point here isn't just the possibility of exact switching, though that seemed to be what was needed to answer Heller's argument. The more important point is simply the possibility of nonconventional things having had different spatial locations at a given time. We *ordinarily* think that things *could have been* moved around and hence that they could have been in spatial locations other than the ones they actually occupy right now. The essence of this intuition is fully compatible with **M+** and with the general view of things as four-dimensional hunks. So in the absence of a compelling argument that the intuition not be accommodated, I think it should be. The intuitive movement of something like a sphere is accommodated in our view of things simply by the phenomenon of the absorbing regions of different *t*-slices of the sphere having appropriately different spatial coordinates.

Somehow or other, *stuff* accounts for the key difference between Heller's position and my own. For it is *as if* Heller's nonconventional things aren't *really* made up of specific stuff, even though he wants to think of a physical object as the material content of a region of space-time. Instead it is *as if* the objects are really just certain *regions*, regions that *happen* to have a certain undifferentiable property, perhaps the property of *being filled* or *being stuffed*. It seems this way for two reasons. First, because the boundaries of a region of space-time *are* uncontroversially essential to it. And, second, because it seems so obvious that the very stuff that there is could have had a different spatial arrangement. Even Heller's choice of terms like "material configuration" (p. 56) and "physical structure" (p. 57) suggests that the regions have somehow supplanted the objects, since these terms admit readings on which the actual *matter* involved is left out of account.

In the ontology of **M+** we are avowedly not talking about various stuffed regions, we are talking about the things that the stuff in various regions constitutes. These things could have had spatial locations other than the ones they actually have.

Could they also have had different temporal locations? The possibility of a *thing* having a different spatial location was seen to depend on the intuitive possibility of *stuff* being differently located in space. So if there were a parallel intuition that *stuff* could be differently located in time, there would be little or nothing to bar the parallel conclusion that a *thing* could have a different temporal location, and we would wind up disagreeing with Heller on both fronts. But I don't think there is any such intuition – at least not a sound one. I do think, however, that there *is* an intuition that might lead the unwary in that direction. I now want to show that the substance of *that* intuition may be retained without forcing the conclusion that stuff could have been differently located in time, so that in the end we are better off agreeing with Heller that things have their temporal boundaries of necessity.

The intuition in question is the thought that a given parcel of *stuff* may *persist* through time (while possibly undergoing relocation in space). That means it may exist at more than one time, and perhaps even constitute the very same object at more than one time. (After all, there would be no "material" difference between such constituted objects.) But this suggests that the stuff, and so perhaps "the object," could have existed at *other* times, since its persistence history might have been somewhat different. And this may open the door to the grander conclusion that it might have existed at *entirely* different times. If we were to follow the original intuition about stuff persisting, we could develop a theory in which *things* could genuinely and plausibly be said to persist through time. Such a theory (let's call it **T**) might be just as adequate for describing the world as **M+**. But I think it would have a serious practical flaw.

The trouble is this. Such a theory seems very much in tune with common sense, which clearly regards familiar things like tables and dogs as persisting through time. But the accord is illusory. By far most of the objects that we *ordinarily* think of as persisting through time aren't like **T**'s genuinely persisting objects at all – they *aren't* constituted by what we might intuitively think of as "the same old stuff" at all the various times of their existence. So cases of ordinary uncritical "persistence" are generally not matched by cases of genuine persistence. For example, consider a table. In deciding which object of **T** is the table, we will simply be *wrong* if we pick *any* of **T**'s genuinely persisting objects. Worse, among those genuinely persisting objects, there are very few that we would ordinarily view even as *objects*, much less as persisting objects.

The incongruity of the theory **T** with ordinary notions of persistence is clearly undesirable, but it isn't enough to overthrow any original intuition about the possibility of stuff persisting. So maybe we should adopt **T** anyway, and view the incongruity merely as an inconvenience. But I don't think so, because I think there is room to accommodate the original intuition without adopting **T**. Here is how.

Suppose that A is a t-object and B is a t^*-object, with t and t^* distinct. Suppose that, intuitively, we want to say that A and B are constituted by the very same stuff (and that some thing or other is constituted by that stuff at all times between t and t^*). I claim there is ample room to capture this intuition within **M+**, and therefore without identifying A and B. Let us say that an instantaneous object x is *homogeneous with* an instantaneous object y iff x and y are (intuitively) constituted by the same stuff. And then, to generalize, we may say that a temporally extended object is *homogeneous* iff all of its t-slices are homogeneous with each other. The "sameness" of the stuff simply does not compel us logically to say that the *objects* it constitutes from time to time are identical. So the fundamental intuitive notion that shows as persistence in one theory shows as homogeneity in the other. (Though of course **M+** would not be committed to there being actual instances of homogeneity.) The world of objects is carved up very differently, but the original "same stuff" intuition is accommodated. In **M+**, ordinary objects like tables are almost always *nonhomogeneous*. In theories like **T**, they are almost always *nonpersistent*.

So, back to the question of whether an object could have had a different temporal location. It seemed that there was no intuitive basis for an affirmative answer unless we were tempted by the possibility of genuine persistence. But since the genuine persistence allowed in a theory like **T** has nothing to do with the ordinary, everyday notion of persistence, it isn't supported by our everyday persistence intuitions. So nothing is lost if we rule it out. Moreover, we have seen that everyday "same stuff" intuitions may be captured in the form of a notion like homogeneity. Any thought that homogeneity doesn't quite measure up to the motivating intuition probably stems from the idea that it somehow falls short of "identity," whereas we have apparently been talking about *the very same, identical stuff* in different spatial and temporal locations. But genuine *identity* is a relation between *things*. To the extent that the motivating intuition was fundamentally about stuff, and not covertly about the things such stuff might constitute, it could not have been either an intuition about identity "of stuff," or one automatically authorizing claims of identity of any constituted things. Something like homogeneity of things is the most it could reasonably have authorized.

Finally, there is this. The thought that a thing's *spatial* boundaries might have been different was in essence the product of an everyday intuition that we have chosen not to abandon: the intuition that (ordinary) things could have been moved around *in space*. Of course, "moving things around in space" has a certain complicated official analysis with respect to **M+** – one that differs strikingly from the corresponding "persistence" analysis. But if the conditions of the official analysis had been met, say, in the case of this table a moment ago, then various mereological sums would have had different spatial locations at the present moment.

Now, in contrast, we have chosen to regard a thing's *temporal* boundaries as essential. This reflects an everyday intuition that parallels the one above, but points in the opposite direction: the intuition that we *cannot* take an (ordinary) thing and move it around *in time*. If we could move things around in time, then we might have (recently?) moved a specific thing around in time, with the result that various mereological sums would have been differently located in time. But since we lack such an intuitive counterfactual possibility, the basis for regarding an official thing's temporal boundaries as inessential is much weaker. It must somehow be extrapolated from a claimed, intuitive, *actual* phenomenon of the persistence of stuff, as we have just discussed at length. In short, there is no solid *counterfactual* intuition providing evidence that a given official thing could have had a different temporal span. So the asymmetry in our treatment of spatial and temporal boundaries is matched by an asymmetry in our everyday thinking about spatial and temporal features of ordinary things. As we will soon see, it is not a consequence of the essentiality of temporal boundaries that, say, a *house* could not have had a different temporal career. This exactly parallels the fact that mereological essentialism does not entail that a house could not have had different parts.

7. AN ALMOST EMBARRASSINGLY SIMPLE ARGUMENT

Peter van Inwagen has argued against certain theories allowing temporal parts – those that take the temporal boundaries of things to be essential to them. He refers to this feature of temporal parts as their *modal inductility* (and *incompressibility*).[6] He writes:

> But then the argument against [the theory] is almost embarrassingly simple. If [the theory] is correct, then Descartes is composed of temporal parts, and all temporal parts are modally inductile. But Descartes himself is one of his temporal parts – the largest one, the sum of all of them. But then Descartes is himself modally inductile, which means he could not have had a temporal extent greater than fifty-four years. But this is obviously false, and [the theory] is therefore wrong. (p. 253)

This is very reminiscent of the house example of Section 4. There, an intuitive modal feature of "the house" is claimed to conflict with a universal modal principle that is endorsed by our theory. Here, an intuitive modal feature of "Descartes" is claimed to conflict with a different universal modal principle that is also endorsed by our theory. There, I argued that to infer the falsity of the principle (and so the theory) would be to commit the Fallacy of Reference with respect to the term 'the house'. Here, I say the same thing: To infer that the principle (and so the theory) is wrong is to commit the fallacy with respect to the term 'Descartes'. In the former case we find an instance of the fallacy involving an apparent (abbreviated) definite description. In the latter we have an instance of the fallacy involving a proper name. Let us briefly discuss the case without benefit of a particular theory of proper names. (Such a theory is reserved for later.)

Here is a diagnosis that shows how the Fallacy of Reference is involved. First notice that **M+**, along with the doctrine that temporal boundaries are essential, doesn't automatically tell us anything about Descartes. It only tells us that the temporal boundaries of things are essential to them. For this to apply to Descartes, there must first be some *thing* that is referred to by the name 'Descartes'. But to think that there is such a thing is precisely to commit the Fallacy of Reference. At the same time I think it is true that some thing *d is Descartes*. But I think this means some thing *d* has the property *being Descartes*.[7] (Of course I am here acquiescing with

[6] van Inwagen (1990*a*), p. 253.

[7] The idea that a sentence like '*d* is Descartes' may feature the 'is' of predication rather than the 'is' of identity has been considered before. Fred Sommers (1969) discusses it in the context of traditional syllogistic, and Michael Lockwood (1975) finds authority for it in, of all places, Mill.

van Inwagen in the shockingly un-Cartesian assumption that some four-dimensional blob of mere matter has this property.)

So suppose with me that '*d*' really does denote some four-dimensional parcel of stuff, a thing ranged over by the quantifiers of **M+**. Then, according to me, to think that the sentence '*d* is Descartes' is an *identity sentence* is again to commit the Fallacy of Reference. According to my theory, the 'is' here is the 'is' of predication, and the sentence itself *only* expresses the proposition that a certain thing, *d*, has a certain property. Now this thing *d* definitely does have the property of modal inductility (and incompressibility). It necessarily endures for a very specific interval of about fifty-four years, and that's it. There are no other temporal possibilities for it.

The intuition that Descartes could have had a longer or shorter period of existence is surely no more to be questioned than the intuition that the house could have had somewhat different parts. So I accept it, and our ultimate theory will accommodate it. But even in advance of a precise theory, it is easy to say what makes the intuition true. It is simply the fact that many mereological sums *other than d* could have had the property *being Descartes*, and some of these entities have longer or shorter temporal careers than *d*. (Of course, they too have their temporal careers essentially.) A full presentation of the theory will of course include a discussion of the nature of such properties as *being Descartes*.

Despite his apparent conclusion that these theories of temporal parts are simply wrong, van Inwagen later admits that there is room for a possible reply. But in order to make it, a proponent of the theory

> . . . must adopt a counterpart-theoretic analysis of modal statements about individuals. And he must suppose that there are two different counterpart relations that figure in our modal statements about the object *X* that is both the person Descartes and the largest temporal part of Descartes: a *personal* counterpart relation and a *temporal-part* counterpart relation . . . while every temporal-part counterpart of *X* has the same temporal extent as *X*, some personal counterparts of *X* have greater temporal extents than *X*. (pp. 253–4)

Van Inwagen sees this as a satisfactory reply for those who find counterpart theory satisfactory in the first place. He concludes finally that those who accept temporal parts (along with essential temporal boundaries) are committed to a counterpart-theoretic treatment of statements of the present kind (p. 254).

But this analysis also commits the Fallacy of Reference. It does so by assuming that "the person Descartes" is *identical* with the entity X, thus forcing questions about what are intuitively Descartes's modal properties to be questions about the properties of the entity X. Hence it becomes necessary to be able to say of X that, qua person, *it* could have had different temporal boundaries even though, qua temporal part (i.e., mereological sum), it could not. If we allow ourselves to be forced into this corner, then recourse to counterparts may indeed seem our only plausible option.

But of course there is no need to be cornered in the first place. Instead, we may simply deny that the sentence 'X is Descartes' is an identity sentence. This avoids the fallacy, and with it the counterparts. We interpret intuitive questions about what properties *Descartes* may have, *not* as questions about what properties X may have, but rather as questions about what properties may be had by *any* thing that has the property of *being Descartes*. One of the properties a thing having this property may have is the property of enduring for more than fifty-four years.

It is important to see clearly that I am not just accepting the counterparts while rejecting the counterpart-theoretic terminology. In a genuine counterpart-theoretic approach there would be an entity denoted by 'Descartes', and that entity would have counterparts in various worlds. On the present view there is no entity denoted by 'Descartes' in the first place. There is of course an entity, say X, with the property *being Descartes*. And there may be another entity, say Y, that isn't, but might have *been Descartes*. But of course Y is not a *counterpart* of X in anything like the sense in question. For one thing, Y is an inhabitant of the actual world, just like X. For another, there is so far no appeal to worlds other than the actual world.

Let us therefore regard **M+** as extended by the addition of the principle that all things have their temporal careers essentially. This is easy to do formally with the help of a new definition:

(*i*) A region r *includes* a time t ('Irt') iff

$$\exists p(p \in r \ \& \ tc(p) = t).$$

(*ii*) A thing x *includes* a time t ('Ixt') iff

$$\exists r(Arx \ \& \ Irt).$$

(Recall that absorbing regions must be unique.) Now we simply add the following as a new axiom:

$$\forall x \forall t\{Ixt \supset \Box [\exists y(y = x) \supset Ixt]\}.$$

Intuitively, thing includes a time if and only if it exists (at least) at that time. So the axiom says that if a thing exists at a time then it exists at that time essentially. From now on we regard this axiom as included in **M+**.

8. STATUES AND LUMPS OF CLAY

In Section 1, I promised to return to the question of whether there might be good reason to think that more than one thing could occupy precisely the same region. In Section 4, I considered the idea that a house and a certain mereological sum were distinct physical objects occupying exactly the same spatiotemporal region, and called it *mysterious*. But the general idea may yet have merit since there may be more compelling examples.

So let us consider an example than which no more compelling example can likely be conceived. Then let us ask whether it is compelling. Suppose that by a miracle a clay statue should suddenly pop into existence, endure for a time, and then just as suddenly cease to exist. Now surely we have a temporally extended entity that it is fair to call a statue. And we have a temporally extended entity that it is fair to call a lump of clay. Do we have one entity or two? If we have two, then it is clear that we have distinct entities occupying exactly the same spatiotemporal region.[8]

The best reason for thinking we have two entities is that we are inclined to say that the lump has properties that the statue lacks. For instance, the lump might have been cubical in shape, but no such possibility exists for the statue. If the lump had been cubical, then either there would have been no statue at all, or else (in a very liberal esthetic spirit) we would have had a (numerically) different statue.

Various responses are possible. Alan Gibbard, for example, holds there is just one entity and embraces an analysis according to which the statue and the lump are identical, but the identity is

[8] The example is adapted from Gibbard (1975).

contingent. Robert Stalnaker is moved to suggest an *actualist* "version of counterpart theory that permits one to make sense of contingent identity and distinctness – that is, of the claims that one thing might have been two, and that distinct things might have been identical."[9] Heller sees the case as good evidence for his "conventional objects," holding that the modal difference between the lump and the statue, since it isn't grounded in physical facts about the object, must be grounded in convention. For him, there is only one genuine (i.e., "nonconventional") object in the region.[10]

It is hard to deny the intuition that there is only one thing in the region. But there is no need to go to extravagant lengths to maintain it. On my view there is but one thing in the region. It has the property of being a lump of clay. It has the property of being a statue. It could have had the property of being cubical, in which case it would still have had the property of being a lump of clay, but would not have had the property of being a statue (or perhaps it would have had the property of being some other statue). There are no mysteries or extravagances here. There is no contingent identity. There are no counterparts. There are no conventional objects. There are just things and their properties.

What drives these writers to extravagance is the Fallacy of Reference. They are taking the expressions 'the lump' and 'the statue' (etc.) to refer to specific things, thus generating the worrisome questions about identity. But, on the present view of things, the sentence 'The statue is the lump' merely says that some thing has both the property *being the statue* and the property *being the lump*. This proposition is of course contingent, but it doesn't assert an identity, so at least it doesn't create those particular worries.

As I urged in Section 5, I think *identity* is just the trivial, absolute, and necessary relation that each thing bears to itself and to no other thing, and that it is extravagant to hold otherwise. So the thing with the property of being the lump and the property of being the statue is, on this view, identical with itself and necessarily so. Had it been the lump and not been the statue, it still would have been identical with itself. Had it been widely scattered and so neither a lump nor (dare I assert?) a statue, even then, it still would have been identical with itself. Had its molecular structure been arranged so that it wasn't even made of clay, or even made of

[9] Stalnaker (1986), p. 122. [10] Heller (1990), chapter 2, section 1.

atoms, it still would have been identical with itself. Under no circumstances would this thing have been identical with anything other than itself. Undoubtedly there are some relations that behave in some respects like identity but which do not hold of necessity. I believe it is a fundamental error to think that one of these relations actually *is* the identity relation, that is, to think that identity actually *doesn't* hold of necessity. I also believe it is seriously misleading to *agree* that none of these relations is the identity relation, but nevertheless to dub one of them "contingent identity."

Heller's view is commendably less extravagant. In fact, it's very like my own. When I say an apparent denoting expression *doesn't really denote*, Heller instead says it denotes a conventional object. Since he also wants to say that these conventional objects *don't really exist*, the difference threatens to be merely terminological. But it isn't. Heller writes:

> There really are no [spatiotemporally] coincident objects: there are just sometimes different conventions applicable to a single physical object. The objects that do exist do not have the modal properties that we commonly think they have. Those putative modal properties are founded on our conventions, not on any actual properties of the objects. What really exist are hunks of matter filling up regions of spacetime. (p. 32)

Let's consider this in light of the example. One of the putative modal properties of the statue is that it couldn't have been cubical. According to Heller, this is *not* a genuine property of the hunk of matter that fills up the region in question, but rather is somehow the product of our conventions. *The statue* is a conventional object, and one of the conventions we have about statues is that they can't be very seriously distorted and still be the same statue. But on my account, this *is* a genuine property of the hunk of matter that fills up the region in question. To say that the statue couldn't have been cubical is to say of that very hunk of matter (among other *things*) that *it* could not both have been the statue *and* been cubical. (The property of *being that statue* is incompatible with the property of *being cubical*.) In my view, it is at least mildly extravagant to treat properties that we ordinarily view as real properties of real things *instead* as properties that *fictitious* things have *by convention*, when there is ample room to treat them as real properties of real things. In order to do so we need only take seriously the idea that certain expressions that we have long thought of as denoting expressions actually are not. In other words, we need only avoid the Fallacy of Reference.

The contrast between Heller's view and mine may be drawn a little more sharply if we think of an example not involving an artifact. Artifacts are not the only "conventional objects." For example, a *planet* is a conventional object, for it has the essential property of orbiting a star. (Mars would cease to be a planet if it stopped orbiting a star, even if it maintained its corporeal integrity.) But now imagine a world containing no convention makers. Intuitively, such a world could include some planets. Intuitively, it is just a brute *physical* fact about such a world that it includes planets. And so it is on my account: Such a world contains at least one thing that has the property of *being a planet*. Heller of course must deny that such a world literally contains any entities that are planets. (In fact he must also say the same of our world.) But since no conventions have been made in that world, he must *also* deny that it contains any merely conventional objects, planets or otherwise, even in the nonliteral sense in which conventional objects may sometimes be said to exist. So it looks like the closest he can come to an intuitively suitable astronomical inventory is to offer something like the following counterfactual claim: If we (or other similar convention makers) were inhabitants of that world and had our *actual* conventions there, then it would be a world in which there were planets (in the nonliteral sense in which conventional objects may be said to exist). This seems to me to be a fairly extravagant departure from intuition.

3

Some properties of things

In this chapter we will consider in detail certain properties (and sorts of properties) that things may have. It is already clear that our theory of names will depend heavily on the ultimate treatment of properties like *being Descartes* and *being Hesperus*. One promising thought is that these properties are "haecceities" (or "primitive thisnesses"). It will turn out that this is not so, but the discussion will nevertheless begin with a consideration of the matter of haecceities. In the remainder of the chapter we will analyze and characterize a number of very closely related properties (and kinds of properties). Many of these properties are easily confused or conflated with one another, hence the discussion may at times seem tedious. But I think the detail is justified because it provides the groundwork for the analysis of the properties that concern us most. It will also serve to reveal that the realm of properties (and thus the realm of propositions) is a good deal richer than we might have previously supposed. The actual analysis of names will be reserved for the following chapter.

1. HAECCEITIES

A familiar argument in favor of haecceities or (primitive) thisnesses goes like this. Suppose the world consisted only of two globes – globes that were "qualitatively indistinguishable."[1] The globes would be at a certain distance from each other. They would be made of the same kind of material. They would be of the same size, color, density, and so on. We can certainly imagine that even at the microscopic and subatomic levels, there was no "qualitative

[1] Black (1952) may have been the originator of the globe example. He used it to argue against a version of the principle of the identity of indiscernibles.

difference" between them. Yet, the argument continues, it seems clear that the positions of the globes might have been reversed. But this intuition, if it really is one, won't make good sense unless there is *some* way in which the globes differ. Since the hypothesis rules out the possibility of *qualitative* difference, any difference must be *nonqualitative*. So each globe must have a nonqualitative feature that "makes it" the globe it is. Such a nonqualitative property is called a *haecceity* or a *thisness*. Some philosophers have found this argument persuasive, but others have simply rejected the intuition that distinct situations have been described in the first place. (In effect, Mark Heller does this in the closely related argument we discussed in Section 2.6.)

It is hard to know what to make of this argument without first knowing what is meant by 'qualitative difference'. The official doctrine of this book is that *things* are made of *stuff*. Accordingly, each of the two things described in the argument is made of a definite quantity of stuff, and obviously the two must be made of entirely different stuff. Is this a qualitative difference? If it is, then the idea that two things could be qualitatively indistinguishable seems absurd. There will always be a qualitative difference between any two things, since any two things will always be constituted by different stuff. If the property *being made of such and such stuff* is a *quality*, then it looks like the argument cannot get started.

But perhaps it isn't a quality. Robert Merrihew Adams suggests a conception of qualities that would rule it out. He writes:

> We might try to capture the idea by saying that a property is purely qualitative – a suchness – if and only if it could be expressed, in a language sufficiently rich, without the aid of such referential devices as proper names, proper adjectives and verbs (such as 'Leibnizian' and 'pegasizes'), indexical expressions, and referential uses of definite descriptions.[2]

This conception apparently has the consequence that qualities must be *general* properties – properties that could be had by different things. For it seems impossible to imagine that a property could only be instantiated by a certain particular thing and yet that it could be expressed without using any of the indicated referential devices. The property *being made of this stuff* is certainly not general

[2] Adams (1979), p. 7. See also his subsequent efforts toward a nonlinguistic characterization of suchnesses, pp. 7–8.

in this sense. There is no serious hope of expressing it without something amounting to the indexical. Moreover, it is clear even without a linguistic test that it isn't general. A *thing*, on the present view, *is* nothing more than the stuff of a precise, fully occupied region. It acquires its status as a thing only as a consequence of our decision to quantify over it. We have taken the view that this very stuff could have had a different spatial location (but could not have had a different temporal location). From this perspective it is preposterous to think that we could quantify over this very stuff and yet be quantifying over a different thing. So the property *being made of this stuff*, on the present view of *things*, cannot be general. Yet I will ultimately maintain that it is a perfect candidate for being the haecceity of the thing in question. Along the way I will be out to question the commonly assumed link between *qualitativeness* and *generality*.

It will prove useful to mention a distinction at this point. We began the discussion with the example of the *globes* but went on to talk about *things*. Naturally, if someone thinks the example concerns two things and that each of them is *identical with* one of two globes, this distinction will not seem important. The things will be qualitatively indistinguishable iff the globes are, the things will have haecceities iff the globes do, and so forth. But this is the Fallacy of Reference. On the present metaphysical view, we may properly say only that the example concerns two things (each of which is of course identical with *itself*) and each has the property *being a globe*. To say that the example concerns globes is *merely* to say it concerns things that have this property. We will see that this has a profound effect on how we should think about the matters before us.

So let us return to the question of whether qualities must be general. We already saw that the property *being made of such and such stuff*, considered as a property of official *things*, could not be general. If this is enough to show it isn't a quality, and if haecceities *must* be nonqualitative, then it is a very plausible candidate for being the haecceity of the thing that has it. Despite the fact that I agree it's an excellent candidate, I want at the moment to shed a little doubt on the idea that generality is necessary for being a quality. I will do this from the point of view that has standardly (and unquestioningly) been adopted in discussions of these matters, namely, from the point of view of the Fallacy of Reference.

Let's use the name '*P*' for the property of *being made of such and such stuff*, and imagine that we are talking about the stuff of one of the two globes. Now focus on a very small, perhaps minute part of this stuff, and consider the property *being partly constituted by that stuff*. Call this new property '*P*'. Then it is clear that *P entails* P^*, in the sense that it is necessary that anything that has *P* also has P^*. Now, embracing the fallacy, let '*A*' denote *the globe* that has property *P*, and let '*B*' denote the other globe. Then it is intuitively clear that globe *B* might have had property P^*. That is, a small fragment of the stuff of globe *A* might have been part of the stuff of globe *B*. Hence the property P^* is *general* in the present sense.[3] It might also be possible to make a case that even the property *P* is general with respect to "globes," but I will not try to do that here. Instead I am content to make the weaker claim that if a general property is nontrivially entailed by a nongeneral property, then the latter property's lack of generality should not *alone* disqualify it from being a quality. (In the case at hand this seems especially fitting, since it is tempting to see *P* as being somehow "composed of" lots of general properties like P^*.)

So there is room to view *being made of such and such stuff* as a genuine quality, and the prevailing, fallacy-driven tendency to see (for example) globes as *identical with* certain *things* may even seem to favor the view. Does it clash with some deeply entrenched usage or intuition? I am not sure. What is the source of the intuition of "qualitative indistinguishability" in the first place? Perhaps there is an intuitive idea that the qualities of a thing are the properties that would be discovered by an ideal, complete investigation of that thing. Then it would be easy to think that two separate such investigations of two different things might not turn up any difference, thus creating the pressure for (nonqualitative) haecceities. But I think this is actually wrong. It should be uncontroversial that, for example, *being made of such and such gold* is one of the *properties* that a certain thing may have, a property that may be discovered in an investigation of the thing. I would say the same for *being made of such and such stuff*. So it belongs on the investigators' list. I grant that

[3] Notice that P^* is also general on the official account of things, since it is already had by more than one thing in the actual world. But on a stricter conception of generality it need not be. For example, if generality required possible instantiation by a distinct, entirely nonoverlapping thing, then P^* would not be general.

it is such an *obvious* property that it could easily be overlooked, but having said this, let's be sure it gets on the list. The problem is simply that the investigators are not in a position to say whether the corresponding entry on the second list picks out the same property. But this is just an accidental epistemic problem. The investigators would not have the problem if the two items were present at the same time. (They would know that the gold (or stuff) of the one thing was different from that of the other because they would observe that it was differently located.)

For the purposes at hand it is not vitally important to decide whether *being made of such and such stuff* should count as a *quality* of the thing that has it. What is important is that the property is a perfect candidate to serve as a thing's haecceity *whether we say it is nonqualitative or not*. (So we should be willing to detach the normally presupposed requirement of nonqualitativeness from our conception of haecceities. And the intuitive notion of qualitative indistinguishability should be understood as carrying the proviso *if examined separately*, or some such.)

This candidate does everything we could reasonably ask of a haecceity: It is an essential property of the thing that has it. It is necessary that if anything has the property, then that thing is the thing that actually has the property. To the extent that it makes sense to speak of other possible worlds, and to the extent that there is any need to "ground" talk of "identity across possible worlds," this candidate fills the bill. So I nominate it for the office.

I think the nominee has a further major virtue. Appeal to haecceities has often been regarded as a desperate measure, one primarily designed to save an uncertain intuition. Desperate, it is said, because it is an *ad hoc* appeal to what are fundamentally mysterious entities – better to let the intuition go. I think some conceptions of haecceities have invited this criticism, but the present one does not. There is nothing mysterious about the idea that things are made up of stuff. And there is nothing mysterious about the idea that the stuff over here is different from the stuff over there. So there is nothing mysterious about the property *being made of this stuff*. In fact it has a very down-to-earth character compared to such proposed haecceities as *being this thing* or *being identical with this thing*.[4]

[4] Robert Adams is mindful of the problem of mysteriousness yet settles for what I think is a relatively mysterious account. See Adams (1981), p. 17.

These properties either cry out for a "soul" or else they have an aura of circularity. They *are* mysterious.

It might be held that I have merely transferred the problem to the arena of stuff – that I offer a nice analysis of the haecceities of things, but it depends on the modal properties of stuff. Conveniently, I have taken the notion of stuff as primitive, and have in effect asserted axiomatically that stuff could have been elsewhere (but couldn't have been else*when*).

This is largely correct. I see what I am doing as putting the problem where it belongs but (honorably) refusing to address it. The problem of the globes, seen as a problem about official things, is fundamentally a problem about stuff. If it makes good sense to say of stuff that it could have been differently located, then we really have imagined two different worlds (even if our epistemic resources are insensitive to such differences). Moreover, we really have seen how it is that the two *things* differ. I claim great intuitive plausibility for the idea that stuff could have been differently located, and I claim the right to regard this as a primitive feature of the primitive notion of stuff. This is not to make the matter a mystery, nor is it to evade the issue in any reprehensible way. There are no theories without primitive notions, and every primitive notion is something that has been left at least partly unexplained.

The alternative, taking *haecceities* as primitive features of *things*, is also legitimate as far as this goes. The difference is that it has an air of mystery (or of the *ad hoc*) because there is no *independent* intuition on behalf of such properties. The intuition that there really are two possibilities for the globes is explained on my account and unexplained on the primitive-haecceity account. And although what explains it is taken as primitive, there is a *separate* intuition directly in support of that primitive notion. So I think the analysis of haecceities in terms of stuff has much stronger intuitive support than the strategy of taking them as primitive.

2. SINGULARY CATEGORIALS

Because previous discussions of haecceities have been conducted under the influence of the Fallacy of Reference, it has been natural to think that if the thing that is the globe has a haecceity, then so does "the globe," and of course it must have the very same haecceity. So phrases like 'the property of being this thing' and 'the property of being this globe' have been used interchangeably in the effort to pick out a certain haecceity. But of course this is wrong. Since 'the globe' is not, properly speaking, a denoting expression, there is no thing that it denotes and about whose haecceity we may worry in the first place. On the present view, what we *ordinarily* think of as "globes" (and the like) are indeed to be found among the things that exist, but this is *officially* just to say that some of the things that exist have the property of *being a globe*. To go further would be to commit the fallacy. Of course the things in the world that have such properties *also* have haecceities, but it would be a double disaster to think of the haecceity of *the thing having the globe property* as the haecceity of *a globe*. The first reason has just been given. The second reason is this. If there were "globes" in the required sense and they had haecceities, then the haecceity of a *given* globe would be the property of *being that globe*. But nothing could have *this* property without being a globe. (It is incoherent to imagine that something might have the property of *being this globe* without being a globe.) But of course the same *stuff* could have been arranged in such a way that the very same *thing* was not a globe.

Despite all of this, I do recognize and rely on a property that might easily be mistaken for the haecceity of a "globe." Suppose '*T*' is a "rigid" name of a thing that is a globe. Then I believe there is a property of *being that (particular) globe*, or *being the globe that T happens to be*. Call this property '*P*'. *P* is of course a property that things other than *T* might have had. Something could have had *P* and yet not have included a few of *T*'s molecules, for example. *Being that globe*, in the present sense, is an extremely important property about which I will have more to say soon. But first let me guard against a potential confusion. Suppose we point at a globe and say "Consider the property of *being that globe*." Here the demonstrative "that" is tied to a specific ostention of a temporal part of a thing that is a globe. Nothing like this went on in our original introduction of the property *P*, even though at one point we used the word 'that'. This at least raises the possibility that the properties are themselves distinct, and in fact I will later try to show that they are. But let me now adopt a simplifying convention. When we are considering any property that is introduced by a specific ostension of a temporal part, I will add a superscripted "o" to the demonstrative. When we are instead considering a property like *P*, introduced without the ostension of a temporal part, I will use an unsuperscripted demonstrative. Although I will discuss the matter more thoroughly below, we may for the moment think of the properties *being that globe* and *being that^{0} globe* as follows. The latter property involves an ostention of a specific *proper* temporal part of a globe. The former does not, but it is *as if* there had been an ostension of the *entire* four-dimensional object (say by God, from a perspective outside of space-time).

Ultimately I will call properties like *being that globe* and, for that matter, *being that^{0} globe*, "rigid singulary categorials." I discuss the notion of *rigidity* below. We now turn to the concepts of *singularity* and *categoriality*. A property is called *singulary* iff it can be instantiated by at most one thing, that is, iff it is impossible for more than one thing to have it. This is to be understood so as not to rule out the possibility that different things could have the property. An example of a singulary property is *being president (of the United States at time* t). Another example is this. Consider the *general* property *understanding Kant*. It may be that only one person has this property. But maybe no one does, and maybe many do. It doesn't matter, because there is still the related *singulary* property *uniquely understanding Kant*. This property is instantiated iff exactly one person understands Kant. This phenomenon is of course perfectly general. For any general property there is a closely associated singulary property which may or may not actually be instantiated. (Some, like *being the only married person*, are necessarily uninstantiated.)

A general comment about definite descriptions is in order here. As we all know, a Russellian theory of descriptions ultimately breaks them apart in the contexts of the sentences containing them. A description like 'the man in the corner' gets broken (in part) into a piece expressing the property of *being a man*, a piece expressing the property of *being in the corner*, and a separate uniqueness claim involving the further expression of these same two properties. But notice that if one accepts an abundant view of properties, as described in Section 1.2, this Russellian account will seem wrong. To see why, first note that not only is there the property of *being a man* and the property of *being in the corner*, there is also the property of *being a man in the corner.* So the sentences 'Smith is a man in the corner' and 'Smith is a man and Smith is in the corner' must express distinct (though necessarily equivalent) propositions. The former attributes a certain single property to Smith, but the latter attributes two distinct properties to him. Similarly, the sentence

'Smith is the man in the corner' should not receive an analysis in which the property of *being a man* and the property of *being in the corner* get expressed as just described. Instead it should receive an analysis according to which a single, and *singulary* property – *being the man in the corner* – is attributed to Smith.

Next we turn to "categorial" properties. A property is (a) *categorial* iff it entails a property that may be expressed by a predicate of the form '*is a*(*n*) . . . ', where the ellipses are to be replaced by a common noun or noun phrase. Properties expressed by predicates of the form '*is* . . . ', where the ellipses are replaced by an adjective or adjectival phrase, are not categorial unless the predicate may be converted to the "article-noun" form without a change of meaning. The predicates 'is a house', 'is a dog', 'is a German Shepherd dog', and 'is a red house' all express categorial properties.[5] Later we will be in a position to associate a "category" with each categorial property. (A consequence will be that houses, dogs, and German Shepherd dogs all form categories, but red houses do not.)

So the property *being that globe* is a singulary categorial. It is singulary because at most one thing can have it. It is a categorial because it entails the property *being a globe*. It is not the haecceity of any *thing* for two reasons. First, it isn't the property of being made of any specific stuff. Second, different things can have it in different worlds. And it isn't the haecceity of "a globe" because to think it is would be to commit the Fallacy of Reference.

Being that globe, or *P*, is very important nevertheless. *P* is whatever property any thing must have in order to count *intuitively* as "the same globe" in different possible circumstances. It is worth emphasizing that if *x* is the thing that *actually* has the property *P*, the fact that in another possible circumstance *y* might have property *P*, and so would count intuitively as "the same globe as" *x*, does not entail that *y* is identical with *x*. We will say more about the exact nature of the property *P* in the next section.

Now suppose the globe is on the table and no other globe is. Then the property *being the only globe on the table* ('Q') is also a singulary categorial, but Q is not the property *P*. Q could be instantiated by a thing that, intuitively, lacked the property *P*. In preanalytic talk, a *different globe* could have been the only globe on the

[5] Categorial properties are obviously closely linked to what are often called "sortal" predicates. Categorial properties are expressed by sortal predicates.

table. Nor is *P* the same property as *being the globe we are now considering* ('*R*'), and for essentially the same reason. (Of course *R* is also a singulary categorial.)

In an intuitive sense, soon to be made more precise, properties *Q* and *R* are not *rigid*, whereas property *P is*. This is already suggested in the characterization of *P* as whatever property a thing must have in order to count as "the same globe" *in different possible circumstances*. There may be "readings" of the phrases we used to pick out *Q* and *R* that are rigid in the same way. (If so, I think they are subsidiary readings.) Now let 'Q^*' denote the property of *being the globe that is actually the only globe on the table* and let 'R^*' denote the property of *being the globe we are actually now considering*. Then I claim that even if Q^* and R^* are acceptable interpretations of the phrases introducing *Q* and *R*, these rigid properties are still distinct from the nonrigid properties that I claimed are *primarily* picked out by those phrases. The rigid character of Q^* and R^* is signaled by the presence of the adverb 'actually' in the phrases we used to pick them out. (The same effect may be achieved by using phrases like 'in fact' or 'happens to be'.)[6] Although Q^* and R^* are rigid in the same way as *P*, we will see that neither is the same property as *P* (nor are they identical with each other).

So I think that under normal circumstances, demonstratives like 'that' (including 'that°') have a rigidifying effect. Roughly speaking, they mandate a certain regularity across worlds that would otherwise not be required. We have seen that what are intuitively "different globes" can have property *Q* (or *R*) in different worlds, but this is impossible in the case of property *P*. No other "globe" can possibly *be that globe*.

But now consider the property *being this red house*. In a normal kind of case, the sentence 'This red house could have been blue' will be counted true. So we are talking "rigidly" about a *house* but are *not* looking *only* at worlds in which it is red. The demonstrative turns a blind eye to the noncategorial component *being red*. A similar thing happens with 'This° waiter could have been a bartender' (again in a normal sort of case), and also with 'This° waiter could have been out of work', but notably *not* with respect to the categorial *waiter*. In these cases the categorial that is rigidified is the

[6] David Kaplan calls such terms "rigidifying operators," but he is of course writing under the influence of the Fallacy of Reference. See Kaplan (1989), p. 577.

property *being a person*. The other entailments of *being this° waiter* are unconstrained (unless they are also entailed by *being this° person*). We may think of the "category" of *houses* as being associated with the property *being this red house* and the category of *persons* as being associated with the property of *being this° waiter*.

Assuming this phenomenon is general, we may perhaps capture it as follows. Let p be any actually instantiated singulary categorial, and let p^* be any *nonsingulary* categorial. Then p^* is the (*rigid categorial*) *core* of p iff (*i*) p entails p^*; (*ii*) no thing in another world could count as the thing that *actually* has p unless it also counted intuitively as "the same (instance of) p^*"; and (*iii*) for any (nonsingulary categorial) p', if p' satisfies (*i*) and (*ii*), then p^* entails p'. Thus if p^* is the core of p, then no thing in another world can be the thing that *actually* has p unless it has the property *being that* p^* (in the given world). So if p^* is the core of p, then the category associated with p is the category of p^*s. (The question of the ontological status of categories – for example, whether they are best seen as classes, as properties, or in some other way – is not important for the purposes at hand. I should also note that an ultimate treatment of the notion of core would probably allow for the core of a given property to vary with context. But such niceties are certainly best avoided here.)

Let's look at some examples. First consider *this° clumsy right-handed waiter*. Intuitively (though perhaps it is not very likely) he could have been an *unemployed but deft left-handed diamond cutter*. In such a world he would still have been the same person though neither clumsy, right-handed, nor even a waiter. The core of *being this° waiter* is the nonsingulary categorial, *being a person*, and accordingly the only properties an instance of *being this° waiter* need "retain" from world to world are those entailed by *being this° person*.

Now consider anew the singulary categorials Q and R. Each of them entails the nonsingulary categorial *being a globe*. But this property does not meet condition (*ii*) of the characterization of *core*, and nor does any other nonsingulary categorial entailed by either property. Hence neither has a rigid categorial core. A thing in another world can have either property without counting intuitively as "the same" *anything*. Of course this is the desired result. If a singulary categorial *has* a (rigid categorial) core, we will call it *rigid*, and we will refer to such properties generally as RSCs.

Now we again consider *P*, the property of *being that globe*. It entails, for example, the nonsingulary categorials *being a globe* and *being a solid*. Suppose we are considering an assertion of the form 'That globe could have had property *X*'. For it to be true, there must be a world in which that globe exists and has *X*. Now, in any world where we find that globe, we find both a globe and a solid. ('That globe could have been a cube' is false.) But the property of *being a globe* entails the property of *being a solid*, so the latter property cannot be the core of *being that globe*. In fact its core is *being a globe*. (And the associated category is the category of globes.)

For a final example, consider *being this red house*. It entails the categorials *being a house*, *being a red house*, and *being a structure*. We have already seen that this red house doesn't have to be red in other worlds. It does have to be both a house and a structure. But since the former entails the latter, the core is the property of *being a house*. Houses form a category, red houses do not. (This is not to say that in a different example *structures* could not form a category.)

3. OSTENSION

Now is a good moment for the further comments about ostension that were promised earlier. It will help if we temporarily suspend worries about the Fallacy of Reference, and use terms like 'refer' in an everyday, intuitive way. We normally think of ourselves as pointing at, nodding toward, and otherwise physically indicating things like people, houses, globes, and the like. But we do not really do this, not if **M+** is a good way of looking at things. The things we normally gesture at are really only brief temporal parts of people, houses, and globes. These are perfectly everyday sorts of things, but they are not people, houses, or globes. It is easy to overlook this because these very gestures, directed at things that are not people or houses, enable us to *refer* to people and houses, the people and houses of which they are temporal parts. Thus I am going to reserve the word 'ostend' (etc.) for cases in which the entity *ostended* is one whose temporal career is necessarily the same as that of the act of ostension. So in a typical case, we manage to refer to a house by ostending a brief temporal part of a house. We do not, in a normal sort of case, also *refer* to the ostended part. If I say "That$^{\circ}$ house needs paint," I only refer to one thing, a house, and I only ostend one thing, a brief temporal part of a house. At the intuitive level, the difference is that the sentence is "about" the thing referred to and not about the thing ostended. Despite this, I believe both entities are "constituents" of the proposition expressed, and I will say more about this later. (In a less normal case we may ostend and refer to the same thing; for example, in 'That° house-slice is red'.)

The role of the ostension in producing the reference is this. It helps picks out a property, the property of *being that° house*, and the entire sentence asserts (partly) that some thing has that property. But that property is a singulary categorial, so only one thing can possibly have it. It is that thing that is referred to in the sentence.

It will help to simplify certain matters that follow if we pretend that ostensions of the kind we are discussing are instantaneous. In reality, they are not. When we point at a house and say "That° house needs paint," or whatever, the part of our action that consists of the pointing together with the utterance "that° house" takes a brief interval of time. So the ostended *thing* – a temporal part of a house – has a certain nonzero temporal thickness. But it will be convenient to pretend it is a mere *t*-part of a house we are ostending.

4. A PARTIAL ANALYSIS

We are now in a position to give a partial analysis of certain RSCs. In particular, we will have something to say about each of the following properties:

(1) P: *being this globe*
(2) P°: *being this° globe*
(3) P^{*}: *being the globe that actually has* t-*part* τ
(4) Q^{*}: *being the globe that is actually the only globe on the table.*

It will be useful for discussing some of these properties if we make a certain temporary assumption, one that will receive fuller discussion in the next chapter. Let us assume that we may introduce proper names for *things* in a way that is independent of their membership in certain categories. By this I mean that we may introduce a name of a thing that happens to be, say, a dog, but that when we use the name counterfactually, we still refer to the same thing regardless of whether it is a dog. Thus we will have names that *rigidly* designate certain mereological sums, regardless of how they happen to be configured in other possible worlds. Introducing such names is easy. For example, we may say "Let '*N*' be a name of the mereological sum that happens to be that° dog." The effect of such a dubbing would be quite different if we had instead said "Let '*N*' be a name of that° dog." For example, the counterfactual form 'If N had not been a dog, then . . . ' would be appropriate if '*N*' had been introduced in the former way, but not if in the latter. We now turn to a discussion of the properties mentioned above.

(1) *P* is the property of being a certain specific (entire) globe, a property that different things can have in different worlds, but only one thing can have in any given world. As we see from Section 3.2, it is an RSC (as are the other properties on the list). Now let '*T*' rigidly denote the thing in the actual world that happens to have *P*. Then, for example, it seems that the thing that is all of *T* except for a few specific molecules could have had *P*, and in those circumstances *T* would not have been a globe at all. Instead it would have been a scattered object having a globe as a proper part.

What is required for something other than *T* to have had property *P*? Intuitively, the thing must not only be a globe, it must be a globe that stands in a fairly intimate relation to *T* itself. Perhaps it has to have a healthy overlap of parts with *T*. Perhaps it also has to have begun to exist at roughly the same time as *T*. Perhaps it has to have been made by the same method, or in the same globe foundry, or in accordance with the same plan, or by the same artisan, or whatever. I don't claim to know exactly what this intimate relation is. Furthermore, I think it is highly unlikely that any very specific candidate would survive careful scrutiny. Any specific candidate is likely to yield some unintuitive consequences, or at least to yield consequences that some would find unintuitive. And any candidate is likely to encounter problems with vagueness. So the project of trying to say precisely what it takes for something other than *T* to *be this globe* in another world seems to me to be distinctly unpromising, and I won't undertake it.

But I still take very seriously the fact that there are absolutely clear cases in which a different thing would *be this globe*, and would be so because of its relation to *T*. Thus I will assume that to have the property *P* is to be a globe that bears a certain relation to *T*, and I will pass up the opportunity to say *exactly* what constitutes that relation. But I will sometimes emphasize the importance of the relation by referring to P as 'P_T'. It seems clear that P_T cannot be a simple, unanalyzable property, and also that it must be a property that T has in the actual world. So it looks like P_T must be some complex, relational, singulary property.

We may generalize as follows. Let C be any nonsingulary categorial, and let x be any thing that actually has property C. Then, with respect to x, there is a certain property that we characterize intuitively as "*being this* (or *that*) C." Let us call it 'C_x'. Then x has C_x and, if y is any object in any world, then y counts intuitively as *this* C iff y has C_x. In the case of *this globe* I dodged the issue of exactly what the property P_T is, and I do the same for arbitrary categorials. I do think there is probably no *uniform* analysis of C_x for arbitrary C. That is, I think the different categorials are likely to display individual eccentricities. I also think that what I said earlier for globes holds across the board: Our concepts are incomplete, there is vagueness to worry about, and no specific proposal for any specific categorial is going to seem clearly right. So a final, complete analysis would most likely have to be to some extent conventional, and to that extent arbitrary. Despite all of this, we *do* speak as if there are definite properties of *being this globe*, *being this table*, *being this person*, and so on. So let us assume for simplicity that where our concepts are incomplete, idealization by convention would be appropriate and reasonable. But, again, we are leaving that task for other hands. For present purposes we will act as if we are dealing with specific, "complete" properties.

It should be noted that the present idea of what it takes for something to have (e.g.) P leaves open the possibility that something that does not actually exist could have P. In fact it leaves open the (unlikely, I think) possibility that something that has *no parts at all that actually exist* could have P, and, moreover, could do so in a world containing no parts of T. Possibilities like these have posed a problem of semantic analysis for *actualists* who accept them but do not accept the existence of "merely possible objects." *Possibilists* have simply bitten the bullet. I don't believe in merely possible objects, so I have some responsibility to say how it is that these things can be possible. I won't do that here. But note that nothing I have said about properties like P makes any commitment to mere *possibilia*. In fact, what has been said about such properties is compatible with the austere view that only things that actually exist could possibly have them.

The problematic case just imagined requires a further comment. Suppose that in some world that contains no parts of T, there is a thing x, none of whose parts *actually* exist, and yet we want to count x as *this globe*. That is, we want to say that x has P_T. In what sense can P_T then be a *relational* property, with T as a presumed parameter? The answer is that it is a *modal* relational property. An example may help. Suppose that our way of thinking about certain globes attached no importance to the stuff they were made of but attached great importance to the foundry that made them and to their ordinal position in the series of that foundry's globes. Perhaps T is the first globe actually made by the Atlas Globe Foundry, but the foundry could have made a first globe, x, from completely different material, and could have done so in circumstances in which the material of T didn't even exist. This surely seems possible. Under those circumstances x would have had the property *being the first globe of the foundry whose actual first globe is* T. This is a relational property with the parameter T. It is "modal" since it involves the notion of actuality.

A final observation about the property P is the following. Suppose that in another world w there is an object y (distinct from T) with property P. Imagine further that someone in w introduces (nonostensively) "the property of *being this globe*" with respect to y, and calls that property 'G'. Is G the same property as P? I believe it isn't. The reason is this: T is the actual globe. So it's clear that T and y are enough alike to warrant the claim that they both have P.[7] But they *are* different, and only a certain amount of difference can be guaranteed to leave us with "the same globe" as we move from world to world. It is entirely possible that in some further world there is an object z that is enough like y to be "the same globe as" y, but *not* enough like T to be "the same globe as" T. So z should count as having property G but not having property P. Thus it seems to me that the relational notion *being the same globe as* cannot be transitive. Furthermore, it may not even be *symmetric*. To say that T is "the same globe as" y is merely to say that T has the property "*being this globe*" *that is associated with* y. Accordingly, to say that y is the same globe as T is to say something quite different – that y has a certain property that is intimately associated with T –

[7] Likeness here may of course extend to the sharing of relational properties involving further entities.

something of potentially divergent truth-value. So whereas y has property P (*ex hypothesi*), it may nevertheless be that T does not have property G. Whether it does must depend on the nature of the case. (Since globes are fairly simple, relatively homogeneous objects, it is actually rather unlikely that we could find a convincing case in which T lacks G).

(2) Now let us turn to the property P°, the property of *being this° globe*. This property is tied to a specific ostension of a *t*-part of a globe. Hence we might think it would more accurately be called the property of *being the globe that has this° part*, but this would be a mistake. For there is nothing to prevent what is intuitively some *other* globe from possibly having this° part. But clearly we want P° to be a property that could be instantiated only by what is intuitively the same globe, plus or minus the *t*-part in question (and perhaps other parts as well). This is achieved if we construe P° as the property of *being the globe that actually has this° part*. Then, for all that has been said so far, there could be a world in which some globe has the relevant *t*-part, but lacks property P°, while what is intuitively *our* globe has P°. (The point is not that there really is such a possibility, only that a correct construal of P° does not rule it out.) Now let us use the symbol '@' as a unary "actuality" operator on formulas. It means *it is actually the case that*. Suppose, as above, that the thing T that has the property P (*being this globe*) is the thing a *t*-part of which was ostended in introducing P°. Then P° may be analyzed as follows:

$$x \text{ has } P^{\circ} \text{ iff}$$

$$x \text{ has } P_T \;\&\; @\exists y(y \text{ has } P_T \;\&\; y \text{ has this}^{\circ} \text{ part}).$$

Now suppose someone makes the imagined ostension, saying "Let 'P°' denote the property of *being this° globe*." (As before, the ° doesn't figure in the utterance in any way, but is only there to remind *us* of the ostension.) And suppose that at a later time someone else does essentially the same thing with respect to what is intuitively the same globe. Does the second person pick out the same property as the first? It may seem obvious that the answer is affirmative, but I take the other view.

It would surely seem obvious that the answer is affirmative to anyone who holds that the globe is simply a three-dimensional object that is "entirely present" on both occasions. For then the distinct demonstrations would be directed toward the very same thing. And since the three-dimensional conception is embedded in everyday common sense, it is natural for *anyone* to think at first that the answer is affirmative. But in a theory of temporal parts – like **M+** – the two ostensions are of distinct (and generally nonoverlapping) things. The part of the globe that is present now and available for ostension is entirely distinct from the part that was present five minutes ago.

It is genuinely obvious that the property P^o entails the property P (assuming we are dealing with what is intuitively the same globe). So anyone who thinks the two imagined ostensions pick out the same property will of course think that property is none other than P. And anyone who, like me, thinks the two ostensions pick out different properties will think neither of them picks out the property P. I think P^o is distinct from P because I think it has a "constituent" that P lacks. I think the ostended *t*-object is a constituent of P^o but not of P. In saying this I rely on an informal idea of the constituents of properties, but it is an idea that I will now try to motivate in discussing the property P^*.

(3) P^* is the property of *being the globe that actually has* t-*part* τ. We are assuming that 'τ' is a rigid designator of a particular mereological sum. Let us also assume that in discussing P^* we have in mind what is intuitively the same globe as the one we have been discussing in connection with P and P^o. Then we may analyze P^* as follows:

$$x \text{ has } P^* \text{ iff } x \text{ has } P_T \;\&\; @\exists y(y \text{ has } P_T \;\&\; P\tau y).$$ [8]

Of course this analysis is only partial because we have declined to analyze P_T. The analysis is certainly correct at the intuitive level. To *be the globe actually having* t-*part* τ is, among other things, to *be this globe*. Furthermore, nothing could *be the globe actually having* t-*part* τ unless it was actually the case that something *was this globe* and had *t*-part τ.

But someone could accept the analysis and still maintain that P^* is identical with P. For notice that P entails P^*: To have P is to have a certain property, namely P_T, that a certain actual thing, namely T, actually has. And as we saw earlier, no thing other than T could

[8] Recall that '$P\tau y$' means that τ is part of y. (See Section 2.3.)

have been the actual thing having P_T. (For otherwise we would be considering a different "*being this globe*" property.) Of course T has all of its parts of necessity. So τ is necessarily a part of T. Since T is actual, it follows that τ is actually a part of T. So the fact that something has P entails that it is actually the case that something has the part τ. Thus P entails P^*.

But this just means they are necessarily coextensive. It doesn't follow that they are identical. Of course, some people accept the principle that necessarily coextensive properties *are* identical. For example this principle has sometimes been adopted, whether for reasons of convenience or of doctrine, in the practice of formal semantics. It makes life easier, but I don't think it squares with ordinary intuition. I think ordinary intuition takes *being a plane equiangular triangle* and *being a plane equilateral triangle* as distinct properties. It even takes an argument to show they're necessarily coextensive, just as it did in the case of P and P^*. Intuitively, the property *being equiangular* is a "constituent" of one of these geometric properties but not of the other. In like manner, *being such that something actually has part* τ is a constituent of P^* but not of P. We may also say, derivatively, that the entity τ is a constituent of P^* but not of P.

It may help seal this to consider the following. Suppose we are still talking about the same globe, but that the property in question is P': *being the globe that actually has* t-*part* σ, where σ is a different *t*-part of the globe. Intuitively, this is a different property from P^*, one that we might well find out was necessarily coextensive. It is a different property from P^* simply because σ is a different thing from τ. But of course if P^* and P' are different from each other, then they are both different from P. The necessary coextensiveness of P^* (and P') and P is misleading but irrelevant.

Now we return briefly to the case of P°. It is arguably identical with P^*. Certainly they are necessarily coextensive, and certainly τ is a constituent of P° in just the way it is of P^* (however that might ultimately be analyzed). This is enough to show that P° isn't identical with P even though the two are necessarily coextensive (like P^* and P). This is all I really care about. It happens that I'm inclined to think that $P^\circ = P^*$, but I can imagine a case for the opposite conclusion. It could be held that the *ostension* somehow exploits unspoken features of τ that must ultimately figure as constituents of P°, whereas P^* pulls τ into the picture in a totally featureless way. For present purposes, this issue in the philosophy of demonstratives is best set aside.

(4) Now we turn to Q^*, the property of *being the globe that is actually the only globe on the table*. Suppose as before that T has the property P and that it is actually the only globe on the table. Now suppose that some thing x has Q^* in some other world W. Then clearly x has property P. This explains how one might have thought that Q^* simply *is* the property P. But the fact that x has Q^* entails that there is *actually* a globe on the table, namely T, while the fact that x has P does not. So Q^* entails P but P does not entail Q^*. The properties are therefore distinct. Now let's try to capture the matter symbolically. We will use 'Tx' to mean *is the only globe on the table*. Then, for any object x (in any possible world):

$$x \text{ has } Q^* \text{ iff } x \text{ has } P_T \,\&\, @\exists y (y \text{ has } P_T \,\&\, Ty).$$

Since the thing T actually has P_T and is actually the only globe on the table, we see that T has Q^*, as desired. But of course in another possible world, some thing x may have Q^* without being on the table.

To summarize: P is distinct from P^o, P^* and Q^*. Q^* is distinct from P^o and P^*. But it might be that $P^o = P^*$. Whether the identity holds depends on how we answer a subtle question about demonstratives. All four (or three) properties are necessarily coextensive.

4

A theory of names

1. THE STANDARD VIEWS

Saul Kripke is well known for having criticized theories of proper names in the style of Frege's and Russell's – theories that hold that there is, associated with any proper name, some definite description (or perhaps a "cluster" of descriptions) that determines the referent of the name (if it has one.)[1] (Some of these views also hold that the description gives the "meaning" of the name, but this thesis is not Kripke's main target. Such theories often maintain that names are "disguised" or "abbreviated" definite descriptions.) There are many different possible theories that could be characterized this way. For example there is much room for variation on the question of the exact nature of the association of description(s) with name. In *Naming and Necessity*, Kripke argues persuasively against some of these variations. His arguments are widely known and have been much discussed, so I will not try to recapitulate or extend them here. I think the arguments are motivated by sound intuitions and that they are essentially correct. But I also think they are shaped by an erroneous presupposition, one that motivates theories of "direct reference" – the main rivals of Frege–Russell-style theories. This motivating presupposition is of course the Fallacy of Reference.

Theories of direct reference hold that names refer *directly* to their referents. But what does this mean? Some have thought it means that names refer to their referents without the aid of any semantic mediation, for example by definite descriptions. David Kaplan rejects this interpretation. He writes:

[1] The most comprehensive presentation of Kripke's position may be found in Kripke (1972, 1980).

The "direct" of "direct reference" means unmediated by any propositional component, not unmediated *simpliciter.* The directly referential term goes directly to its referent, *directly* in the sense that it does not first pass through the proposition . . . When the individual is determined . . . it is loaded into the proposition. It is this that makes the referent prior to the propositional component . . . [2]

Something like this seems right, at least if we employ a little charity with the ambiguous word 'determined' (etc.). In a sentence like 'The tallest spy lives in Venice', the "semantic material" that "determines" the referent is part of the very proposition expressed. But now consider 'Wilt lives in Venice'. Certainly there is a perfectly good sense in which the name 'Wilt' might have its referent "determined" by a definite description, say if the name was explicitly introduced into the language by appeal to a description. But that description doesn't contribute anything (other than its referent) to the proposition expressed. Wilt himself is a *constituent* of the proposition. Thus *rigid designation*, or something very close to it, is a corollary of this account of direct reference. Kaplan writes:

If the individual is loaded into the proposition (to serve as the propositional component) before the proposition begins its round-the-worlds journey, it is hardly surprising that the proposition manages to find that same individual at all of its stops . . .[3]

But alas, in supposedly paradigm cases like 'Wilt lives in Venice', it *doesn't.* Not if "individuals" are simply certain occupants of spatiotemporal regions. The proposition (in general) finds different individuals in different worlds. These different individuals of course all have the property of *being Wilt*, but they are nonetheless different individuals, composed (in general) of different stuff. Direct-reference theorists have sought theories of *how names refer* that avoid the errors of the description theories. But to assume that names *refer* in the first place is to commit the Fallacy of Reference.

In contrast, one can imagine versions of the description theory that do not commit the fallacy. An example would be the following elaboration of the Russellian view that names are disguised or abbreviated descriptions. If 'Aristotle' is just an *abbreviation* of the description 'the teacher of Alexander', then the sentence 'Aristotle loved wine' is, in turn, just an abbreviation of the sentence 'The

[2] Kaplan (1989), in Almog, Perry, and Wettstein, eds. (1989), p. 569.
[3] *Loc. cit.*

teacher of Alexander loved wine'. And if the description *itself* is to be "analyzed out" in context, in the familiar Russellian way, then what survives contains no occurrence of the name – and no occurrence of the description – in search of a referent. So there is no need for a description theorist to hold that names have referents in the first place. *Reference* may be held to be a purely semantical relation holding between certain terms and certain things. Since the unabbreviated, fully Russellized sentences carry all the semantical weight, and since they contain no terms corresponding to names (or descriptions), there is no *semantical* reason for thinking that names refer. So, for example, the theory could maintain that only pronouns (or variables of quantification) refer, and that they do so only under certain very specific conditions. Of course it would be compatible with this to hold that we may, in a *derived* (and loose and popular) way, speak of the referent of (an occurrence) of a name: It would be the thing that some relevant pronoun (or variable) has as *genuine* referent in the unabbreviated and (fully) Russellized variant of the sentence containing that occurrence. (But we will see later that there are dangers in this.) Description theories may therefore be seen as holding that names are "semantically inert" and thus dispensable, while, in sharp contrast, direct-reference theories elevate them to the status of an independent semantic category.

That names do not refer (except perhaps *derivatively*) is the potential grain of truth in description theories. The grain of truth in direct-reference theories is that description theories don't work. The reason they don't work is, very roughly, that they clash with the facts of modality. This is what Kripke showed so forcefully. It is clear that Aristotle *might* not have been the teacher of Alexander, because we can easily imagine actually discovering that he wasn't. It *could* turn out that Alexander's mother was actually his teacher, and that she faked some evidence in order to confer extra prestige on her son. It could also turn out that she disliked wine, whereas Aristotle loved it. It is these sorts of intuitions (and more complex versions of them) that Kripke brings to bear against simple description theories (and more complex variations on them).

It is therefore genuinely ironic that what is wrong with the direct-reference theories that these modal criticisms spawned is that *they* clash with the facts of modality. We now turn to an examination of this claim.

2. A KRIPKE-STYLE THEORY

Here is a rough theory of names that is nevertheless sharp enough for the purposes at hand. The theory concerns ordinary proper names in the ordinary sense of that term, not in some technical sense from semantics or grammar. Thus we are talking about what we would ordinarily classify as proper names: 'Hesperus' and 'Phosphorus'; 'Bill Clinton' and 'The White House'; and 'Superman' and 'Clark Kent'. The theory I want to discuss consists of the following five theses:

(1) We are somehow able to pick out things ostensively. For example we may point and say "this° table."[4] When we do this we apparently often succeed in communicating our intentions to our hearers.
(2) We are able to exploit (1) to introduce names of things. We will call this the phenomenon of *dubbing*. The conferring of a name upon an infant, a dog, a ship, or a building is normally a case of dubbing.
(3) We are also able to introduce names by means of definite descriptions. For example, we might do this by saying "The building to be erected on this site will be called 'The Apex Tower' "; or "The theory of names consisting of theses (1)–(5) will be called '**K**' " – as it will.
(4) Names that have been satisfactorily introduced by either method are "rigid designators" in the sense that when they occur (appropriately) in counterfactual contexts, they denote the same things they denote when they occur in noncounterfactual contexts. This is true even if the name has been introduced by means of a description that does not itself designate rigidly in this sense.
(5) An ordinary occurrence of an ordinary name of an ordinary thing succeeds in referring to that specific thing in virtue of a causal chain of an appropriate sort leading back to an appropriate introduction of that name (or an appropriate ancestor of that name) via method (2) or (3).

I think theory **K** clashes with the facts of modality. Let me say why. Suppose we build an ornate castle in the Napa Valley and dub it, say, 'Château Jubien'. According to the theory, we have named a thing, a specific physical object. But in another world that very physical object might not have been a castle at all. For example, it might be a mereological sum that overlapped a castle but for one of its stone blocks and included in addition a like stone block unconnected to that castle, a part of the adjacent winery. Now someone might say "In building Château Jubien and the winery we used the

[4] Of course, as emphasized above, the superscript is not uttered. It is just a bookkeeping device for the purpose of reminding us that the case involves ostension.

same supply of granite blocks, so some of the blocks of the winery could have wound up being blocks of Château Jubien, and vice versa." Here the second occurrence of the name appears in an (appropriate) counterfactual context, the first does not. And, according to the theory, the name is a rigid designator. So both occurrences must designate *the same thing*. It follows that, with respect to any of the worlds satisfying the counterfactual stipulation, 'Château Jubien' designates an entity that, *in those worlds*, is *not* a castle. It is instead a scattered object that is the mereological sum of a proper part of a castle and some blocks that are parts of a winery. But this clashes with the facts of modality. With respect to any such counterfactual circumstance, 'Château Jubien' surely denotes a thing that is a castle (assuming for the moment that proper names denote things in the first place). We want to say that Château Jubien could have had some different parts. This is a pretty brute fact of modality. But, as I urged in Section 2.4, the thing that is Château Jubien could *not* have had different parts. In order to accommodate the facts of modality, we need a different theory of names.

3. ORDINARY PROPER NAMES

Let us begin by confining ourselves to the case of names that we would *ordinarily* say actually denote actually existing (physical) things. (Other cases will be dealt with later.) The theory will combine aspects of both of the standard sorts of theories we have been discussing.

The central thesis of the theory is that proper names do not designate *at all*. Instead they are disguised *predicates* that express rigid singulary categorials. In the next section I will try to say just *which* RSCs such disguised predicates express. We now discuss certain aspects of the theory that do not depend on this detail. The present theory resembles the description theory in that names get "analyzed out" in context. And it resembles theories like **K** in that what is right about the fundamental *rigidity* intuition is preserved through the medium of the RSCs, but in a way that complies fully with the facts of modality. Let's look more carefully at how it works.

When I say that names are "disguised predicates" I have something quite specific in mind. Let me illustrate with an example. The sentence 'Hesperus is a planet' expresses a certain proposition.

According to the present theory, it is the proposition that something has the property of *being Hesperus* and the property of *being a planet*. Using the term intuitively, no particular thing is a "constituent" of this proposition. It is a general existential assertion, an assertion to the effect that something *or other* has each of two specific properties. In first-order notation, this proposition would be expressed by a sentence of the form

$$\exists x(Hx \,\&\, Px).$$

It would not be expressed by a sentence of the form Ph nor by one of the form $\exists x(x = h \,\&\, Px)$. Each of these commits the Fallacy of Reference in one way or another.

This form for understanding declarative sentences containing names will be our norm. It thus reflects the widely held belief that sentences containing names normally express propositions that have existential force as a result of containing those names. But it is quite clear that this is not *always* the case. Sentences that affirm or deny existence using a proper name do not express propositions that assert existence *as a consequence of containing the name*. Otherwise the denials would be contradictory (and the affirmations would be in a certain way redundant). So they must not have the normal form. The proposition that Hesperus exists (e.g.) is instead expressed by a sentence of the form

$$\exists xHx.$$

It would be natural to accompany this with an argument that existence is not a genuine property, but I can't think of a convincing argument for that view, and my "abundant" instincts don't favor it anyway. So I will content myself with the claim that existence is a quasi-logical notion, and that it is properly expressed by the existential quantifier rather than by a first-order predicate. This is of course compatible with the view that it isn't a property, but it's also compatible with the view that it is. It would just be a special, quasi-logical property. I will say more about the difference between the normal case and the exceptions below, where the present theory will be claimed to provide a better account than simple description theories can provide. In a nutshell, the reason is that description theories explain the normal existential force as part of the meaning of the name, but the present theory instead sees it as a presupposition of the context. So I think the name has the same meaning in both sorts of contexts, but evidently simple description theories cannot say the same.

The property of *being Hesperus* is sometimes expressed by the predicate 'is Hesperus', as in the sentence 'The brightest planet is Hesperus'. Since cases like this invite the fallacy, I will borrow Quine's device of hyphenating the predicate and will employ it from now on.[5] Thus, in place of 'Hesperus is a planet' we may write

$$\exists x(x \text{ is-Hesperus} \ \& \ x \text{ is a planet}).$$

Now let us consider the sentence 'Hesperus is Phosphorus'. It does not *explicitly* affirm or deny existence. Yet, on the present view, the occurrences of the names require existential force. This suggests that its proper form must be

$$\exists x \exists y(x \text{ is-Hesperus} \ \& \ y \text{ is-Phosphorus} \ \& \ x = y).$$

An alternative view is that the proper form is the simpler (but necessarily equivalent)

$$\exists x(x \text{ is-Hesperus} \ \& \ x \text{ is-Phosphorus}).$$

This view, I believe, has a fatal flaw: It leaves no room for an intuitively acceptable *negation*. In a normal sort of case, "Hesperus isn't Phosphorus" commits the speaker to the existence of Hesperus and Phosphorus and to their diversity. But there is no way to place a negation sign in the single-quantifier formulation that achieves this effect. In the two-quantifier version, we simply negate the embedded identity formula. (Other placements of the negation sign in two-quantifier formulations accommodate different propositions one might express in unusual circumstances by such sentences. For example, consider 'Michael Jordan isn't *Superman*!'. It is nicely handled by negating the embedded conjunct 'y is-S'. The result is commendably silent on the question of Superman's existence.)

I believe the negation problem is decisive against the single-quantifier treatment. But a second problem is that the treatment

[5] See Quine (1953, 1961), pp. 7–8. There are two substantial differences between Quine's position and the one we are developing here. One is that he is thinking of properties like *being Pegasus* (his example) as *primitive*, whereas we will go on to analyze them. The other is that he is making a technical point about the capabilities of Russell's theory of descriptions, and is not actually commiting himself to the existence of *properties*.

would have to be accompanied by a general doctrine telling us which possible positions of occurrences of names in sentences carry existential import. (Presumably it would be 'Hesperus' that contributed the quantifier in the first example, not 'Phosphorus'.) Such a doctrine might be impressively difficult to state.[6]

The present theory holds that predicates like 'is-Hesperus' express *rigid singulary categorial* properties, and the ultimate analysis of such properties will make this clear. But let us first examine each of the three features separately.

Singulary properties are those that can be had by at most one thing. Ideally, every ordinary proper name would be associated with just one thing. Unfortunately (for semantics), there are lots of people named, say, 'John Smith'. There is room to hold that, despite this, they all have different names, names that happen to be spelled the same way. If this can be defended (as I think it can), then every name *is in fact* associated with just one thing. In any event, it will emerge that on the present theory the property *being John Smith* associated with one person is distinct from the property *being John Smith* associated with another. So the present view either conforms to the surprising facts or else idealizes them in favor of "univocality."

Now we turn to *rigidity*. Properties like *being Hesperus* have nonsingulary categorials as rigid cores. In the case of *being Hesperus* the rigid core is the property of *being a celestial body*. (Note that the core is not *being a planet*, since it seems clear that Hesperus might not have been a planet since it might not have been in orbit around a star.) The rigidity insures that nothing in another world could have the property *being Hesperus* unless it counted intuitively as

[6] Yet another view along the present lines is that ordinary proper names are disguised existential quantifiers of a certain special sort: ones that incorporate a restriction to a certain domain. On this account 'Hesperus is a planet' might have the form [∃ is-Hesperus x] (x is a planet), where the quantifier would be read by "Some is-Hesperus-er x" (or, again following Quine, by "some Hesperusizer x"). The quantifier ranges only over things satisfying the predicate 'is-Hesperus' – we might say it is "singularily restricted." The problem with this approach, I believe, is that it makes proper names *automatically* have existential force, whereas the present view is that when they do have such force, they have it only because it is imposed upon them by the prevailing context. I believe this gives the most satisfying account of cases in which names evidently lack existential force. So I think the question of how to translate (say) 'Hesperus does not exist' into explicitly quantificational form poses a serious problem for the restricted-quantifier view.

"the same celestial body." But what is crucial is that something *could* count intuitively as the same celestial body without literally being the same *thing*, that is, without being identical with the thing that *actually* is-Hesperus. Thus we are able to preserve the Kripkean intuition that counterfactual talk "about Hesperus" is always talk about "the same celestial body" without forcing it to be talk about what is literally the same thing. So there is no clash with the facts of modality of the kind deplored at the end of the previous section.

Finally, *categoriality*. This reflects the fact that we name things "categorially." We say "Let 'Hesperus' be a name of such and such *celestial body*" and the like. (And even if we said " . . . such and such *planet*," the *core* would nevertheless be the property of *being a celestial body*.) The phenomenon of categorial naming prevails even in cases where there is no explicit appeal to a categorial. For example, if we break a bottle of champagne over the hull of a ship and say "I name thee *Neptune*," we are implicitly naming *a ship*. It even holds in cases where there is an incorrect *explicit* appeal to a categorial. For example, it seems that Hesperus is named with respect to the category *celestial body* even if the namer says "Let 'Hesperus' be a name of such and such *star*." The practical effect of the phenomenon of categorial naming is extremely important. It is that subsequent counterfactual talk using the name is infected with the presupposition that the "bearer" of the name instantiates a specific categorial. That categorial is whatever the (rigid categorial) core of the RSC associated with the name happens to be. Here are two examples. The core of *being Cicero* is *being a person*; the core of *being Neptune* is *being a ship*. When we consider situations in which Cicero would have lived in a barn, we do not consider worlds in which he is a cow or a chicken. There are no worlds in which something that is a chicken also *is-Cicero*. When we consider situations in which *Neptune* would never have sailed, we do not consider worlds in which it is a house or a bridge. There are no worlds in which something that is a bridge also *is-Neptune*.

So this is a theory according to which names are not *designators* at all. They disappear (in context) in favor of predicates when the disguises are removed. Any semantic phenomenon *resembling* designation (or "reference") must be accounted for via the semantical activities of pronouns, quantifier words, and quantifiable variables. Of course, if ordinary proper names are not even *designators*, then they cannot possibly be *rigid* designators (nor can they be said to *refer directly*). So the theory, thus officially construed, is sharply at odds with a fundamental Kripkean thesis about names (and with all manner of direct-reference theories).

But an unofficial construal is also available. According to it, we may think of names as designators in a *derivative* sense. Consider the sentence 'Cicero is an orator'. It is a disguised version of the sentence 'Something is-Cicero and is an orator'. It thus entails the sentence 'Something is-Cicero'. Since we are presently only considering names that (intuitively) succeed in denoting, this sentence is true. Moreover, since 'is-Cicero' expresses *being Cicero*, and *being Cicero* is singulary, only one actual thing satisfies 'is-Cicero'. Informally, and derivatively in just this way, we may think of 'Cicero' as denoting that very *thing*. This will work perfectly well if we are only considering nonmodal contexts. But in other possible worlds, *different* things have the property *being Cicero*. So we cannot take 'Cicero' as denoting the same thing in all possible worlds. In a given world, it may denote some other appropriate thing – whatever thing happens to satisfy 'is-Cicero' *there*. This too works perfectly well, preserving the intuitive view of 'Cicero' as a *designator*. But it cannot be a *rigid* designator. So even this informal, derivative construal of names as designators conflicts with fundamental Kripkean doctrine. In what follows I will not hesitate to speak informally of (ordinary proper) names as designators, or of the referents of such names, and so forth. But I will do so only with the clear understanding that they are not *rigid* designators (and, of course, are *designators* only by a courtesy).

It would be easy to overstress this departure from Kripke, and I certainly do not want to do that. What I regard as the truly fundamental insight that led Kripke to the thesis of rigid designation is *not* something that deserves to be rejected. Quite the opposite – it deserves to be preserved, and the present theory preserves it. I think the present theory is precisely where Kripkean intuitions lead when they are purged of the Fallacy of Reference, specifically, when they are purged of the assumption that if a term denotes (in the generous, derivative sense) what is intuitively "the same *person*" (or *ship*, etc.) in another possible world, then it automatically denotes what is literally the same *thing* in that world.

Now, what is the analysis of properties like *being Cicero* or *being Hesperus*? My view has two important features. First, it attaches great importance to actual *namings*, that is, to certain actual events in which names are introduced (whether by dubbing or description). To this extent it is rather Kripkean in spirit. The second feature is that despite the first feature, properties like *being Hesperus* are without exception properties that the things that have them would have had even if no name had ever been introduced. So the exploited aspect of the naming event is not one that depends on there having been a naming event.

I am assuming, with Kripke, that names may be introduced in two ostensibly different ways, by description and by dubbing. So let us consider the cases separately. First suppose that the name 'Hesperus' was introduced by means of a description. Someone might once have said something relevantly like this: "Let 'Hesperus' be a name of *the celestial body that occupied position* p *at time* t." (For simplicity we assume that p and t are such that exactly one celestial body occupies p at t.) Then I claim that the property of *being Hesperus* is the property of *being a celestial body that actually occupies position* p *at time* t. Call this property 'H^*'. (H^* is closely analogous to property Q^* discussed in Section 3.4.) Then I am claiming that the intuitive property *being Hesperus* is none other than the property H^*.

Three comments are in order. First (still assuming that the use of the definite description was successful in introducing the name 'Hesperus' in the first place), H^* is clearly a singulary property. Hence it is unnecessary to retain the 'the' from the ordinary language of the description. At most one thing can have the analyzing property. Moreover, retaining the 'the' would be potentially misleading since it might suggest that the ultimate analysis waits on a further Russellian (or other) decomposition of the retained description, whereas it in fact does not. Second, the analysis uses the *actuality* operator where the ordinary language description did not. The reason is that intuition rules that something could *be Hesperus* without occupying that spatiotemporal position. Finally, if we imagine that the name 'Phosphorus' was introduced similarly but with a *different* description (say one involving a different position and time), we see that the property of *being Phosphorus* will be a different property from the property of *being Hesperus*. (This is a consequence of the further analyses properties like H^* received in Section 3.4.) I think the fact that the properties are different has a significant bearing on Frege's problem about the informativeness of 'Hesperus is Phosphorus', and on such related problems as the opacity of belief contexts. (I will comment on these matters in the next section.) In any event, the present theory sees this sentence as a disguised version of the sentence

$$\exists x \exists y (x \text{ is-Hesperus } \& \ y \text{ is-Phosphorus } \& \ x = y),$$

where the two predicates express distinct properties.

But perhaps it isn't obvious that the intuitive property really is the property H^*. It might be claimed that it is instead the property *being that celestial body* (where the demonstrative is nonostensively directed at the entire thing in question, as in the case of property P of Section 3.4). Let's call this property 'H'. We saw (in 3.4) that the analogous properties P and Q^*, though necessarily coextensive, failed to be identical. Why think that *being Hesperus* is H^* rather than H? The reason is simple, but it is heavily obscured by our intuitive purposes in introducing the name. It is this: In naming by description we exploit a certain property in order to *define* a new term. It cannot be that we are simply "fixing a referent," for we have rejected the Fallacy of Reference – the name does not (officially) *refer* in the first place. It may be that our *intuitive* goal is (in *some* sense) to "fix a referent," but it nevertheless *must* be true that something else is going on. That something else can only be the defining of a new term. For something to *be Hesperus* simply *is* for it to have whatever property it is we happen to exploit in the definition. That's what it *means* to *be Hesperus*. In the present example, it is to have the property H^*.

What clouds this (and makes it easy to think the property might instead be H) is the fact that our intuitive goal is merely to introduce a term that will "pick out a certain thing." This accounts for the inclination to think that any other property enjoyed by the thing would have served just as well in introducing the name 'Hesperus'. And to this extent it would. But on the present account the property of *being Hesperus* would nevertheless then be a different property. Its success in "picking out Hesperus" would be due entirely to its necessary coextensiveness with H^*.

Now let us imagine that 'Hesperus' was introduced in a dubbing. Imagine that someone once pointed at Venus and said something like "Let 'Hesperus' be a name of that celestial body." Continuing to pretend that ostentions are instantaneous, we thus imagine that the person pointed at a *t*-part of Venus. Now what property is *being Hesperus*? One view might be that it is the property of *being that celestial body*, that is, *H*. This is a plausible and natural view, but I think it's wrong. Here is why. There is in fact no celestial body present and available for ostension. What is present and available is a mere *t*-object. We must therefore construe the apparent ostention of an entire celestial body as a *definite description* of a celestial body involving a genuine ostention of one of its parts. So the dubbing just imagined is really a naming by description. It is *as if* the dubber had said "Let 'Hesperus' be a name of the celestial body that actually has that° part." This formulation makes explicit what is implicit in the original, namely the specific object that is in fact being ostended. And, in parallel with the property P° of Section 3.4, it does so in a way that ensures that anything having the property would count intuitively as "the same celestial body," namely by the appropriate inclusion of 'actually'. Note that the original formulation succeeds intuitively because it exploits the fact that the appeal to the categorial has the effect of "bootstrapping" what is in fact merely the *ostension* of a *t*-object into a *reference* (in the derivative sense) to a containing, temporally thicker thing. The improved formulation merely makes explicit what thing is actually ostended, and then adds the actuality operator to capture what is intuitively intended but unstated in the original. The ostension of the *t*-part is embedded essentially in the dubbing event. Without the ostension of *that t*-part we do not have *that* dubbing. This essential ingredient is abandoned if we say that *being Hesperus* is merely *being that celestial body*.

So the present view takes a typical case of dubbing to be an implicit introduction of a name by description, where the implicit description involves a demonstrative reference to a proper part of the object being named. Accordingly, a successful candidate for the property so generated must conform to the general pattern noted above in description cases. Thus the property *being Hesperus* generated by the dubbing can only be the property: *being a celestial body that actually has that° part*. This property is connected to the dubbing through the medium of the actually ostended *t*-part, but is so connected without requiring any dubbing to have taken place. Notice that this departs from the improved formulation of the dubbing only by making the article indefinite. The reason is that the definite article is superfluous since the property is *already* singulary. (A more thorough comment on this matter will soon be offered.) This is the analysis we want. An immediate consequence is that if Hesperus were dubbed 'Phosphorus' on some different occasion, the property *being Hesperus* would be distinct from the property *being Phosphorus*. (Similarly for cases with one dubbing and one demonstrative-free description.)

Now let me turn to two important questions about this account of names. (1) Why don't Kripke-style objections to the description theory also apply to the present theory? (2) Why isn't the present theory just a specific version of the description theory?

(1) It is evident that we "could discover that" Aristotle was not the teacher of Alexander, was not the author of *Posterior Analytics*, and so forth. But suppose he was named in a dubbing involving a certain *t*-part of a human infant. Could Aristotle have failed to have the property of *being a person who actually has that° part*? A satisfactory answer requires a closer look at what is going on in the Kripke-style thought experiments that weigh against the description theory. Using the worlds metaphor, there may seem to be two different ways of characterizing these exercises. One of them makes the present theory seem vulnerable to Kripke-style objections. We will see that it rests on an elementary mistake. But first we will take a closer look at what lies behind the proper construal of the thought experiments.

There are lots of possible worlds. One of them is actual. In the actual world, Aristotle is the teacher of Alexander. So there are no possible investigations that we could *now* undertake in the actual world that would show that he was not. We could, of course, wind up convincing ourselves that he was not. But we would be wrong. We would not have *discovered* that Aristotle was not the teacher of Alexander. So, still assuming that he actually was, there are no possible worlds that *extend into the future* the way the actual world is *so far*, and in which Aristotle does not teach Alexander. So the idea that we "could discover that" Aristotle didn't teach Alexander needs a less literal elucidation against the background of this view of worlds and actuality.

I believe that elucidation should go roughly as follows. Surely there are some possible worlds that are compatible with all we know *that is independent of Alexander's tutelage*, but in which Aristotle does not teach Alexander. *This* is the right way to understand the thought experiment. To say that we "could discover that" not-*p*, in the face of our firm belief – and even knowledge – that *p*, is merely to say that there are worlds in which not-*p* holds that are compatible with everything we know regarding matters independent of *p* (and thus not-*p*). For all we know, matters bearing on *p* (and not-*p*) aside, not-*p* is true. In effect, this is just a worldsy exercise in support of the intuition that *p* is not a necessary truth. The reason it is so effective against the description theory is that no typical proponent of that theory would think, in a typical case, that the relevant *p is* necessary. The problem is that the theory's original proponents didn't notice that their theory committed them to the necessity.

But now notice that it *is* a necessary truth that Aristotle is a person that actually has that° part. On the present conception of the worlds metaphor, there is an abundance of worlds, and one and only one of them is actual. So *any* true assertion of the form '*A* is actually *P*' is necessarily true, since it merely means that *A* has *P in the actual world*. Naturally this does not mean that whatever is true in the actual world is necessarily true. In particular, it is not necessarily true that Aristotle taught Alexander.

To say that there are other possible worlds is to concede that other worlds "could have been actual." This is surely right, but it carries with it a dangerous temptation: the temptation to think that when we say that *p* could have been the case, we are saying it is possible that *p* is *actually* the case. Or to think that when we say that *p* is the case in a (nonactual) world *W*, we are saying that *p is actual* in *W*. And since there are certainly worlds in which Aristotle fails to have that° part, those who succumb to the temptation may wrongly conclude that we "could discover that" Aristotle does not *actually* have that° part. This is the wrong way to construe the thought experiment. In effect it is to think that if we "could discover that" *p*, then we "could discover that" *p* was *actually* the case. So, since we could discover that Aristotle did not have that° part, we could discover that he did not actually have that° part, and the claim that it is necessary that he actually has that° part must be false.

But this depends on an equivocation on the term 'actual' (etc.). Suppose *p* holds in the nonactual world *W*. Then there *is* a sense in which *p* is *actual* in *W*. But in this sense, 'actual' merely means *true*. It is this sense of 'actual' that fuels the move to the incorrect construal. Of course, to say that *p* is actual in *W*, in this sense, is not to say that *p* holds *in the actual world* at *W*. When I claim it is necessary that Aristotle actually has that° part, I do not mean it is necessary that Aristotle *truly* has that° part. If this were what it meant, the word 'actually' would be redundant (and the claim would be false). No. What it means is that it is necessary that in the world that happens to be the one and only actual world, Aristotle has that° part. This is perfectly compatible with the observation that some other world, a world in which Aristotle lacks that° part, could have been "the actual world."

The actual world is not necessarily the actual world. But what goes on in the actual world, or in any other world, goes on *there* of necessity. A world in which Aristotle lacks that° part could have been actual. That would not have made it identical with our world, but would instead have been enough to ensure that our world was not actual. The necessity of intraworld goings-on merely reflects the fact that we take intraworld goings-on as constitutive of worlds. When the goings-on get different, so do the worlds.

In short, *being a person who actually has that° part* is a different property from *being a person who has that° part*. To find a world in which Aristotle lacks the latter property is not to find a world in which he lacks the former. So the usual Kripke-style examples, while devastating to typical description theories of names, do not apply in any straightforward way to the theory under discussion.

(2) But is the theory under discussion nevertheless just a specific description theory? The answer is that it isn't. I think the reason is quite significant, but it is unfortunately somewhat hidden from view. The theory holds that (ordinary) proper names are "disguised" singulary predicates (that express certain singulary properties – RSCs, to be precise). But there are two different kinds of singulary predicates. First, there are those that may be obtained from ordinary, nonsingulary predicates by adjoining to them an assertion of uniqueness. Thus, for example, the singulary predicate 'is the man reading a book' results from the nonsingulary predicate 'is a man reading a book' by replacing the first occurrence of 'a' by 'the', and thus adding a uniqueness assertion.

The second kind of singulary predicate consists of all the rest. These are predicates that contain *no* explicit component asserting uniqueness. They don't need to, because the singularity is already present in the property they express. A good example is the property of *being president* (*of the United States at* t). To assert *that Clinton is president* is automatically to exclude the possibility that someone else is *also* president, because the property is singulary. The property of *being president* is the same property as the property of *being the president*. The 'the' is redundant when the business at hand is merely the expression (or attribution) of the property. It is needed only when the business at hand requires an assertion of existence that isn't supplied by some other sentential component. (As, for example, in 'The president will speak at 9 o'clock'.) But in the case of a mere property attribution, the redundant 'the' is also potentially insidious, because it introduces possibly unwanted existential import.

On a Russellian account of descriptions, combined with a description theory of names, the natural translation of 'Clinton is president' would be something like

$$\exists x[Cx \mathbin{\&} \forall y(Cy \supset x = y) \mathbin{\&} Px]$$

(for some appropriate predicate 'C'). But the translation of 'Clinton is *the* president' must include a further existential quantifier because it contains a definite description. This difference may seem innocent enough in this case, but if proper names are disguised definite descriptions, the door is open for unwanted existential quantifiers when names are used in contexts that do not presuppose existence. This danger does not exist for the present theory because it holds that names are disguised singulary predicates *of the second sort*. So there is no existential force supplied by what names are held to *mean*.

A defender of the description account may reply that there is no real danger in locating existential import in the meaning of names, because that import may always be "canceled" by other elements of the containing sentence. Thus, it would be claimed, in 'Hesperus does not exist', 'Hesperus' has existential force, but the predicate of the sentence serves precisely to cancel it. In 'Hesperus is a planet', the name once again has existential force, but the predicate allows it to stand. This account contrasts sharply with that of the present theory, according to which the name has no such force in either sentence. In the first sentence, the *predicate* supplies a negated existential quantifier. In the second sentence, an unnegated existential quantifier is supplied by the context of the actual tokening of the sentence: roughly, by our common knowledge that Hesperus exists.

So a description theorist would try to deal with cases like 'Hesperus does not exist' by invoking a doctrine of cancellation. But it isn't clear that all such cases display arguable elements of cancellation. Let me try to sketch an example in which it is much less clear that anything like cancellation is present.

We often utilize well-known fictional characters in our talk about *actual* states of affairs. A frustrated detective might say of a tough case: "If Bulldog Drummond were on this case, he'd be able to solve it." Here we have an anaphoric pronoun reaching back across a subjunctive conditional to an "empty" proper name. For a description theorist, the most natural translation into an explicitly first-order sentence is probably something like

$$\forall x[(Dx \mathbin{\&} \forall y(Dy \supset x = y) \mathbin{\&} Ox) \Rightarrow Sx],$$

for a suitable 'D'. (Here we avoid unnecessary complications by letting 'Ox' and 'Sx' mean *is on the case* and *solves the case*. Also, '$\Rightarrow$' represents the subjunctive conditional.) Now, there is surely no existential import here, and that is all to the good. But where is there any *cancellation* of import? There is no negated existential quantifier. Nor is there an existential quantifier lying in the scope of any other operator that could plausibly be held to cancel its existential force. If there is any cancellation going on here at all, it must be a kind of "occult" cancellation. So the doctrine of cancellation will have to be far subtler than might originally have been supposed.

The present theory doesn't have to strain to accommodate this sort of case. The context of this sort of utterance is one in which no existential force is given to the token of the name. So it is no surprise if we find none in the appropriate explicitly quantificational translation. (Whether the ultimate translation would be analogous to the above is a question I will not try to answer here.)

It is important to see that I am not claiming that an ordinary *occurrence* of a name like 'Hesperus' does not contribute an existential assertion to the proposition expressed by the containing sentence-token. It does. The point is that it does not do this as part of the invariable *meaning* of the *name*. The name has a certain invariable meaning that it lends to every occurrence. But some occurrences of the name acquire *further* import from the surrounding context. The invariable meaning of the name is, in effect, just the RSC that the associated predicate expresses. In some contexts this meaning is supplemented by an assertion of existence, in others it is not.

So the present theory is significantly different from description theories. Whether it is significantly better as a result may not be obvious. The Bulldog Drummond example suggests that it is. I also think it is very appealing intuitively to think that it is the actual context of use that settles the question of the existential force of names.

5. FREGE AND SUPERMAN

We now turn briefly to Frege's infamous puzzle about informativeness and the related problem of the opacity of belief contexts. Leaving aside its existential force, the sentence

(1) Hesperus is Hesperus

could never be informative, but this is certainly not true of the sentence

(2) Hesperus is Phosphorus.

This poses an acute problem for those who commit the Fallacy of Reference. For they believe both sentences are *identity* sentences and, at least in the case of direct-reference theorists, that they both express the same proposition. But if they both express the same proposition, how is it that they can differ in potential informativeness? Isn't becoming informed just a matter of coming to know propositions we didn't formerly know?

I will not survey the numerous strategies that have been deployed in addressing the puzzle. I will merely say how it fares under the present theory of names. According to that theory, neither (1) nor (2) is an identity sentence in the first place. (1) has the form

(1′) $\exists x(x \text{ is-Hesperus} \;\&\; x \text{ is-Hesperus})$,

and (2) has the form

(2′) $\exists x \exists y(x \text{ is-Hesperus} \;\&\; y \text{ is-Phosphorus} \;\&\; x = y)$.

Assuming that the introductions of 'Hesperus' and 'Phosphorus' exploited different properties of the mereological sum in question, the predicates 'is-Hesperus' and 'is-Phosphorus' express different properties. So (2′) [and thus (2)] asserts, among other things, that a certain property is instantiated, a property about which (1′) [and thus (1)] has nothing to say. This is enough to show that (1) and (2) express different propositions. On the face of it, if they express different propositions, it should come as no surprise that they might differ in informativeness.

In fact, if we consider the sorts of properties the two names would express in a typical case, it is clear that one could know that each property was instantiated without knowing they were instantiated by the same thing. For, in a typical case, the proposition expressed by

(3) $\exists x \exists y$(x is-Hesperus & y is-Phosphorus)

simply *does not* entail that Hesperus is Phosphorus. (A "typical" case is one in which the names are introduced on separate occasions via properties that could be had by two different things. In atypical cases the entailment may of course hold. A simple example is a case in which we explicitly introduce, say, 'Phosphorus' as "a new name for Hesperus.")

But there is still a question to be raised. In what sense do we "grasp" properties like *being Hesperus* and *being Phosphorus* in the first place? On the present theory, the properties are complicated "modalized" properties having to do with ancient temporal parts of Venus, or with ancient features of its location, or the like. It is clearly incorrect to think that an ordinary person even suspects, much less knows, that Venus has these arcane properties. But surely ordinary people "grasp" (or "understand") names like these on a regular basis. Since the theory claims that the arcane properties are the meanings of the names, not only is the explanation of Frege's puzzle doubtful, but the theory itself must now be questioned.

I believe this criticism evaporates if we take what might prove to be a sobering look at the facts. I do not believe that we should give up the idea that ordinary tokens of ordinary declarative sentences ordinarily express specific propositions, and that different tokens of a given sentence generally express *the same* proposition. It is hard to see how the phenomena of communication, exchange of information, agreement and disagreement, and so forth can possibly take place, as they evidently do, if something like this isn't true. Of course there is room to reject this position, and some philosophers have famously done so. I won't try to show why I think these alternative views are ultimately inferior. I will just assume that the proposition account is the best, and will point out one of its apparent consequences. (Someone who rejects the proposition account is then free to see what I am claiming as a conditional, and may even see its unwelcome consequent as damaging evidence against its antecedent.)

I think it is just an obvious matter of fact that we generally do not really *know* the meanings of all the words that we use when we utter everyday declarative sentences. For example, consider the occurrence of the word 'declarative' in the previous sentence. I don't really know precisely what it means. For example, is it a syntactic notion or a semantic one? It "sounds" semantic, but I seem to remember some grammar school teachers saying some very syntactic things. Were they wrong? If it is semantic, what does it mean? I would say it means *expressing a proposition*. But can this be right? We have just been alluding to philosophers who don't think there are any propositions. But they don't think there aren't any declarative sentences. I may be confused about the precise meaning (or meanings, or perhaps even "vague meaning") of the term, but I do generally know a declarative sentence when I see one. We would all score well on any test that is likely to be given.

Now, it is tempting to think this is just the problem of vagueness in one of its guises: that declarativeness is a vague notion and that my confusion just matches the vagueness and doesn't reflect any real lack of knowledge. But this isn't really right. I don't think I really know the meaning of even such a word as 'meter', in the legislated scientific sense of the precise length, about which there ought to be no serious vagueness. I know there is some precise scientific definition of the word, but I just don't happen to know what it is. Yet I think I can understand sentences containing the word and can successfully express propositions using the word.

I think this means that what we normally call *understanding* or *grasping* propositions or the meanings of words, is a much looser relation than we might previously have thought. It does not require precise *knowledge* of the meaning. (And in the case of vague terms, it doesn't require precise knowledge of the tolerated boundaries, probabilities, or whatever.) So I can be said to grasp the concepts of *declarative sentence* and *meter* despite actually having a certain significant amount of ignorance or confusion. The general fact is that we often don't really *know* what we're talking about, but we manage to understand or grasp it anyway.

Given this view of the matter, there is no embarrassment in the idea that properties like *being Hesperus* are ones that can almost never be pinpointed by competent users of the name 'Hesperus'. They *grasp* the meaning of the name anyway. The consequence for the present view of Frege's puzzle is that someone could genuinely be said to grasp the meanings of both 'Hesperus' and 'Phosphorus', but without *knowing* precisely which properties these names express. This means that even in an atypical case, in which (3) entails (2′), there is room for informativeness with no epistemic lapse on the part of the informed.

We may see this even in the sharpest possible case. Suppose that, by the sheerest coincidence, the actual introductions of the names exploited the *very same* property of the thing. Then the two associated predicates would express the same property. But then (2′) would express the same proposition as

$$(2'') \quad \exists x \exists y (x \text{ is-Hesperus } \& \ y \text{ is-Hesperus } \& \ x = y).$$

Despite this, someone might understand (2′) without knowing that it expressed the same proposition as (2″). And he might be informed by (2′) precisely because his understanding of 'Hesperus' and 'Phosphorus' was insufficient to assure him that they had precisely the same meaning.

Note that the original explanation in the *typical* cases is essentially the same. There the grasp of the informed on the names is insufficient to assure him that they are names of the same thing. The difference is that this would have been so no matter how good his grasp had been, even if he had *known precisely* the meanings of the names.

A problem that is quite similar to Frege's puzzle is the apparent opacity of belief contexts. Lois Lane believes that Superman can fly. Superman, of course, is Clark Kent. So how can it be that Lois doesn't believe that Clark Kent can fly? (To avoid unwanted complexities, let's pretend these characters aren't fictional.)

Well, the answer is that the proposition that Superman can fly is simply a different proposition from the proposition that Clark

Kent can fly, assuming the two names express different RSCs. Hence the sentences 'Lois believes that Superman can fly' and 'Lois believes that Clark Kent can fly' don't express the same proposition, and there is no embarrassment in affirming one and denying the other.

But what if the names have the same meaning by sheer coincidence? Then the two sentences express the same proposition, so they are both true. Our tendency to deny the second and affirm the first, and Lois's tendency to deny 'Clark Kent can fly' and affirm 'Superman can fly' then need explanation. But the explanation is the same as it was for the problem of informativeness. It is that Lois's understanding of the names is insufficient to assure her that they have the same meaning, and even insufficient to assure her that they name the same person. Her understanding of 'Superman' is such that she believes that the person she calls by that name can fly. But the opposite holds for her understanding of 'Clark Kent'. When we (falsely) deny that Lois believes that Clark Kent can fly, we reveal that we suffer a similarly incomplete understanding.

6. NAMING MEREOLOGICAL SUMS

In Section 3.4 we temporarily assumed that we could introduce names of *things* (i.e., *mereological sums*) independently of their membership in any categories, and promised further discussion. It was perhaps a little misleading to "assume" this in the first place, since that suggests that it stands in need of some form of justification. But I think it is obviously true. Others may be happier with a weaker claim that happens to be good enough for present purposes: If we are able to name anything at all, then we can name mereological sums independently of their membership in any categories.

It is important to be clear about the meaning of the independence proviso. It does not mean that we may not utilize a category in order to isolate a specific mereological sum for naming. Thus we may say "Let 'π' be a name of the mereological sum that is in fact the celestial body on the western horizon right now." The categorial *being a celestial body* has been appealed to in the introduction of the name. But our subsequent use of the name does not carry with it any presupposition that the entity it names is a celestial body. We may happily contemplate possibilities in which π fails to be a celestial body. It is in this sense that π has been named independently of its membership in any categories.

We do not ordinarily introduce names of pure mereological sums. We ordinarily have no need for such names. But examples like the present one make it clear that we have all the requisite resources. Names of mereological sums *appear* to work just the way Kripke and direct-reference theorists generally have thought ordinary names work. They seem to be "rigid designators" of things. The thing π is to be found in another world if and only if all of the parts of π exist there, regardless of their mutual spatiotemporal relations. (But recall that a thing may not occupy a different temporal location.)

There are two possible ways to view names of mereological sums that are compatible with what has been said so far. One is to take the direct-reference appearances seriously and view them as irreducible singular terms, terms that may replace variables in the way that individual constants do in first-order logic. On this view, a sentence like 'π is a celestial body' has the first-order form '$C\pi$'. The name 'π' is not a disguised predicate. On this account, in sharp contrast with the present view of ordinary proper names, 'π' may appear in genuine, unanalyzable statements of identity.

The alternative is to say that names of mereological sums do not differ semantically from ordinary proper names. They too are disguised predicates. The difference is that the predicates in question have the further feature that they can only be satisfied by the *thing* that actually satisfies them. In fact there is room to view these predicates as expressing RSCs – we need only decide to accept the property of *being a thing* as a categorial. Then, for example, the RSC associated with the above introduction of 'π' would be the property of *being a thing that is actually the celestial body on the western horizon now*. And the sentence 'π is a celestial body' would be a disguised version of 'Something is-π and is a celestial body', just as in the case of an ordinary proper name. We might call properties like *being* π "relentlessly" rigid singulary categorials, emphasizing the fact that only the very mereological sum that is-π in the actual world could be-π in any other world. But the seeming qualification really adds nothing beyond emphasis, since there is no room for anything but the same mereological sum to count *intuitively* as the same mereological sum. Relentlessness would just amount to the fact that the categorial involved was *being a thing*. (Any RSC where the categorial is narrower will fail to be relentlessly rigid.)

The primary reason for rejecting the direct-reference view of ordinary names was, in effect, that such names cannot be held to denote the same mereological sums from world to world. Since this defect is missing in the case of names of mereological sums, a direct-reference account of them is more plausible. Is it plausible enough? Here it may be helpful to recall Kaplan's intuitive characterization of direct reference. The issue is whether the individual thing is "loaded into" the proposition in advance, or instead is determined anew at each world in accordance with propositional components. With ordinary names it had to be the latter because there was no single entity appropriate for loading in the first place. Here, there is. Then does it get loaded?

There is at least some reason to think it does. Let's consider the question with the help of an example containing an explicit modal operator. The sentence 'It's not necessary that π is a celestial body' provides as good a test as any. Does the term 'π' contribute the descriptive material that was originally used in defining 'π', to the proposition, for application world to world, or does it just contribute the mereological sum itself? Does the proposition (among other things) look to the *actual* western horizon from the "vantage point" of each possible world, or does it simply and strictly have to do with the thing that 'π' names?

Here is a case for the latter conclusion. Consider the result of substituting the defining description for 'π' in the original sentence. The result is a natural language sentence of a *form* that often nicely admits or even promotes a *de dicto* reading: 'It's not necessary that the mereological sum that is actually the planet on the western horizon is a celestial body'. But it doesn't favor a *de dicto* reading here. The placement of the modal operator in the ordinary-language sentence seems irrelevant to the proposition expressed; it might as well have the smallest possible scope. In either case the proposition expressed is openly about a certain mereological sum. In order to engender a *de dicto* understanding, we would have to go considerably out of our way and say something like "It does not hold of necessity that whatever mereological sum is actually the celestial body on the western horizon is a celestial body." In fact even this sentence does not *require* a *de dicto* reading. Thus there is something about the nature of the description that seems to favor the *de re* reading even when the operator appears in prime *de dicto* position.

Certainly the presence of the actuality operator, since it forces us back to the actual world to complete the evaluation, contributes most of the *de re* pressure. But a certain amount may also be due to the fact that the proposition is explicitly about a *mereological sum*. In any event, this phenomenon gives evidence that when the description does not appear at all, but 'π' appears in its place, we have a sentence expressing a proposition that is directly about a particular mereological sum: The entity π has been loaded into the proposition. This in turn supports the idea of treating names of mereological sums like individual constants in logic, and seeing them as paradigm cases of the phenomenon of rigid designation. (This approach has the further advantage of avoiding the somewhat unintuitive idea that *being a mereological sum* is a categorial property.)

But I don't think the evidence for the approach is conclusive. Its nonuniformity with the account of ordinary names clearly counts against it. A closely related disadvantage, which I will not discuss in detail, is that it would apparently require that *things* be "constituents" of (certain) propositions. This would make some propositions "impure" abstract entities, while others would be "pure." On the uniform approach the things would be supplanted by certain properties. Since properties are inevitably going to be constituents, the overall account of constituency would be much smoother.

In any event, let us contrast the above modal example with the parallel case involving an *ordinary* proper name. So consider the sentence 'It's not necessary that Hesperus is a celestial body' (and set aside any possible epistemic construals). Since 'Hesperus' is a disguised predicate, an (undisguised) *de dicto* reading would be: 'It's possible that something be-Hesperus and not be a celestial body'. This reading is perfectly natural and in no way disfavored by the original sentence. Of course, since *being Hesperus* entails *being a celestial body*, the *de dicto* reading is false, but that is beside the present point. That point is merely that such a reading of the ordinary language is clearly available. Of course, so is the *de re*. The sentence 'Hesperus is not necessarily a celestial body' invites it. The *de re* reading is given by 'Something is-Hesperus and isn't necessarily a celestial body'. Of course *this* expresses a true proposition. More will be said about such modal examples in the next chapter.

Let me conclude this section with a comment on a topic I will not discuss in any detail. It seems to me that our general conception of *abstract entities* also fits well with a direct-reference account of their names. Despite this, it seems true that we ordinarily name abstract entities categorially, for example, with respect to such categories as *properties, numbers,* and so forth. What favors direct reference and rigid designators here, though, is the fact that we do not normally think that different entities can, say, have the property *being seven* (or *being the proposition that snow is white*) as we pass from world to world. As in the case of mereological sums, this is not conclusive and the matter of nonuniformity remains a serious concern.

7. EMPTY NAMES

I am a proponent of actualism. So I don't think Superman exists (in any sense of that word). I have read many stories that contain what look like ordinary proper names of people, places, and things. (So far I have never read a story that contained what looked like a name of a mereological sum.) Not only do these apparent names occur meaningfully within their home stories, they occur outside them as well, as in the second sentence of this section. Most of this section will be devoted to names that originate in stories, myths, and the like. But we begin by looking at some "empty" names that are not introduced in stories.

Suppose I am hallucinating. I seem to see an alligator on the floor of my study. I decide to name it. I say, "Let 'Dexter' be a name of the alligator that is now in my study." Have I introduced a name that happens not to have an (intuitive) referent, or have I just failed to introduce a name? If we accept 'Dexter' as a name and extend the present account of ordinary proper names to cover such cases, then 'Dexter' is a disguised predicate expressing the property of *being an alligator that actually occupies my study now.* Nothing has this property in the actual world. Nor is there anything with this property in any other world. There are worlds in which I have this very study at this time and in which the study happens to contain exactly one alligator. But since that alligator isn't actually in the study, it cannot be Dexter. So the expression 'Dexter' is necessarily "empty." But I can't see that it does any harm to view it as a *name* anyway. It looks and behaves like an ordinary proper name in all other respects. For example, in coming to my senses I might reasonably be said to realize *that Dexter does not exist, was a figment of my imagination*, and so forth. So 'Dexter' seems closely analogous to empty expressions from fiction and myth like 'Moby Dick', 'Pegasus', etc. Since it is very difficult to deny that these expressions are names, we do best to grant a similar status to 'Dexter'.

It is possible to concoct names that are empty but *not* necessarily so. Say I am trying to form a club. A law requires that only "registered" clubs may collect dues from members. It also requires that a club must be registered under an official name. I want to collect dues from the members. Also, the club I want to form must have a certain minimum number of members in order to be the sort of club I intend it to be. (For example, a baseball club.) I understand that it is possible that not enough people will want to join the club. So I name it *conditionally*. I say, "If *n* people agree to join a club satisfying such and such description by time *t*, the club thereby formed will be called 'The Barons'." I go register "the club" under the name 'The Barons'. But not enough people agree to join in time. I abandon the project. (Although the law may think The Barons exist, I know better. Perhaps I tell the registry that the club has been disbanded, or even that it never existed. Of course it might be that the law can accommodate this sort of conditional arrangement, thus avoiding possible ontological embarrassment.) A month later I think, "If The Barons had existed, I'd be a nervous wreck by now." Certainly this might be true. So the name is empty, but it isn't necessarily empty. The property of *being The Barons* is, very roughly, the property of *being a club that meets the condition and description actually set forth by MJ at such and such time*. (We want to understand this so that any rigorous formulation would allow the name an intuitive referent only in worlds where I do set forth an appropriately similar condition and description. Notice that this example is independent of the exact metaphysical nature of clubs.)

Now we turn to stories (and the like). Stories appear to contain two sorts of names: names of "fictional" entities and names of actual entities. Actual people, places, and things often appear in works of fiction. *A Tale of Two Cities* is a tale about Paris and London. The Empire State Building looms large in *King Kong*. Plato gets a nod in *The Confidence Man*. Certainly it would be very counterintuitive to think that these works do not refer to the actual people, places, and things that we normally refer to when we use the same names. But thinking that they do is not without problems, two of which will now be mentioned, only to be set aside.

Stories (etc.) apparently attribute actual *properties* and *relations* to things both actual and merely fictional. Often stories seem to say straightforwardly true things about actual entities. A story might contain the sentence 'Los Angeles is almost 400 miles from Sacramento'. Now, Los Angeles *is* almost 400 miles from Sacramento. Is this enough to make the occurrence of the sentence in the story true? It isn't clear. Suppose the 'almost' had been replaced by 'over', and that the story was consistent on this point. Suppose even that a key development in a trial (in the story) depended on the distance being greater than 400 miles. Would the occurrence of the (modified) sentence in the story have been *false*? We are accustomed to thinking that a storyteller is largely entitled to create his own reality. Why can't he set the distance between (actual) cities, at least within limits? If he can dangle a giant gorilla from the Empire State Building, why can't he add a few miles to the trip from Los Angeles to Sacramento? Well, the point is that if he can, then it's hard even to take the *original* sentence as merely expressing the true proposition that the distance is almost 400 miles. If these sentences of fiction are to count as true at all, then there is at least *some* pressure to treat them as expressing propositions other than the ones they express in everyday, sincere, nonfictional contexts. The problem is to treat them so without abandoning the intuition that the names they contain refer to what they refer to outside of fiction. Trying to solve this problem is beyond the scope of the present work.[7] I will simply assume that these names have their usual (intuitive) referents even in fictional settings.

Stories also apparently make reference to actual *times*. A story might contain the sentences: 'It was New Year's Day of 1947, and New York was soaking wet. I still had to tail my suspect.' In conformity with the above remarks, it is by no means obvious that the first sentence is subject to refutation by appeal to the actual weather records of New York City. Yet it seems clear that the words refer to a particular actual day and to the particular actual city of New York. But a factual refutation does seem a bit more plausible when the dating is tied to a notable historical event. For example,

[7] David Lewis (1978) addresses some very important questions about truth in fiction. Some of his conclusions are compatible with mine, some aren't.

consider a story beginning with the sentences, 'Inauguration Day of 1953 found us with the crowd on Pennsylvania Avenue. It poured.' Even if the passage is not from an "historical novel" that makes an effort to "get the *facts* right," there is something about this sort of case that makes a refutation by actual fact seem more plausible. Again, this problem is one I will not address.

In order to consider the matter of naming in stories, let us adopt a certain intuitive perspective that should be compatible with just about any plausible theory of fictional language. Let us assume that stories (etc.), at least many *consistent* stories, depict "worlds." There are various ways in which this might be construed, some of which I want to avoid. In the actual world, and in the diverse "possible worlds" of diverse metaphysicians' fancies, there are no gross indeterminacies, at least at the macroscopic level. Every thin man has a certain weight at every given time in any such world. When I say stories depict worlds I don't mean worlds that have this sort of characteristic "completeness." The world depicted by *The Thin Man* does not "settle" the question of the title character's exact weight at each moment of the story. Perhaps it is misleading to use the term 'world' here for precisely this reason. But I am going to use it anyway. So we have to be careful to understand that a "world" depicted by a story is bound to be somewhat "incomplete" – it omits all the "unsettled" stuff. Semanticists and model theorists might be tempted to think that by 'world' I therefore mean something like *(appropriate) equivalence class of ("complete") worlds* – the class consisting of just the worlds that are compatible with everything that gets "settled" in the story. Properly understood, this might suffice for semantical purposes. But since I believe such an approach is too easily misunderstood, I want to avoid it. So my fictional worlds are in an important sense "incomplete" or "partial."[8] Does this mean they are "fragments" of "complete" possible worlds? To say yes would again be to promote a misunderstanding. The misunderstanding is that worlds in my sense are related to "metaphysically" possible worlds by something like the part–whole (or subset, or entailed-by, etc.) relation. I want to use the term so that it is *neutral* on this question. The reason is that I

[8] Lewis (1978) holds that there is a plurality of "complete" worlds associated with each specific work of fiction. He attributes a "single incomplete world" position like the one adopted here to John Heintz.

will ultimately claim that fictional worlds are ("metaphysically") *impossible*. What this means, of course, is that stories (in the sense of *fictional* stories) *could not be true*. There is no (metaphysically) possible world of which the world depicted in *The Thin Man* is a fragment (even if the novel is perfectly consistent).

Intuitively, the "world" depicted in a story "consists in" all and only what the story "settles."[9] Dramatically different ways of defining (*fictional*) *world* so as to capture this intuition are conceivable. Some might be more acceptable ontologically than others, but, ontology aside, they would be more or less on an equal footing for technical semantical purposes. Another possibility would be to take fictional worlds as primitive. In what follows I will avoid the issue and simply operate with the intuitive notion just characterized.

Now let us imagine a story that contains an explicit naming. Although it is not as likely literarily, let's imagine that it's a naming not involving any ostension. A character, say a scrupulous New York real estate developer, declares, "The building to be completed on the northeast corner of 65th and Madison in the borough of Manhattan in the year 1995 will be called 'The Apex Tower.'" Later in the story the building gets completed and people are constantly talking about the Apex Tower. Some people say things like "Sure it's great, but I wish they had put it on their other site near the East River; it would have been fabulous there. And the one they built on the river would have been fine on Madison." Here we have characters in the story commenting on what might have been for the fictional entity, the Apex Tower. I want to suggest that the property of *being the Apex Tower* is the property of *being a building that is actually completed on the northeast corner of 65th and Madison in the borough of Manhattan (in New York City) in the year 1995*, understood with respect to the world of the story.

Elaboration is in order. Leaving the story aside, consider the property of *being a building that is actually completed on the northeast corner of 65th and Madison in the borough of Manhattan (in New York City) in the year 1995*. This is a perfectly good property, one that

[9] Much of the effort in Lewis (1978) is devoted, in effect, to questions about what stories do "settle." I will avoid the question here, assuming only that consistent stories settle more than what they explicitly "entail," but less than what would be needed for "completeness."

may or may not prove to be instantiated in the actual world. Call this property '*A*'. Then the present suggestion is *not* that (in the world of the story) the property of *being the Apex Tower* is the property *A*. The suggestion is rather that *being the Apex Tower* is a *fictional* property, distinct from *A*, a property that, in the world of the story, would be picked out by the very phrase – italicized above – that picks out *A* in the actual world. They are different properties because in the different contexts the adverb 'actually' picks out different "worlds." In the fictional context, the actuality notion is tied to the world of the story. In the actual world, it is of course tied to the actual world. So, in my view, when the name 'the Apex Tower' occurs in the story, it is a disguised singulary predicate that expresses the *fictional* property just mentioned. In adopting this view I am really only insisting that ordinary names in stories work, *within those stories*, just the way actual ordinary names work in actuality. As a rule, stories are surely *not* about people whose language somehow works differently from the way the language in which the story unfolds works outside the story.

Of course the names of fictional entities do not normally get explicitly introduced in the stories that contain them the way we have imagined 'the Apex Tower' was introduced. No matter. If the fictional entities in a story have *names*, then, in the world of the story, even though it isn't part of the *explicit* content of the story, those names must have been introduced in one of the ways names *can* be introduced, namely, by means of an implicit or explicit description (including dubbings involving ostensions). So the fact that the characters have *names* in the story is enough to justify the claim that the story *settles* that their names were introduced in one of the ways names *can* get introduced. So the names are disguised singulary predicates, but the story simply does not say which specific RSCs they express. As noted in Section 5, this is not very different from the normal course of events in the actual world. Things often have names. These names are disguised singulary predicates. It is rare indeed when we know exactly which RSC a name expresses. Of course this is not a practical problem given our normal uses for names. We generally *do*, in effect, know the relevant "necessary coextensiveness class."

What about occurrences of 'the Apex Tower' outside the story? A critic might say, "I loved the book. But I did agree with Ada [a character] that the Apex Tower belonged on the river. Putting it on

Madison was a serious esthetic mistake under the circumstances." Or, in a different context, we might correct someone's misapprehension (in 1993) by saying, "Oh, the Apex Tower won't *actually* exist. It's only a building in a *story*." What property is expressed by the disguised predicate in uses like these?

To answer this we should first think of what it would take for something to instantiate such a property. This gives a clue, for it is really pretty clear that nothing could. Imagine that, unbeknownst to the author of the novel, *The Apex Tower*, a project with lots of the key fictional characteristics was in fact under way. It would be completed in 1995 on the site in question and would be called 'the Apex Tower'. The developer responsible would have the same name and lots of the same features and motivations as his fictional counterpart. The similarities could be so striking that no publisher would dare touch the book, even though it could be documented that it was written by someone while shipwrecked on a remote island in the South Pacific, utterly out of touch with the New York real estate scene. It cannot be seriously maintained that the actual Apex Tower is the fictional Apex Tower.[10] (Nor could such a thing be maintained if the author had instead been a real estate insider who knew all about the project and wanted to base a novel on it. Then his Apex Tower would be the actual Apex Tower, not a fictional entity. Much of what he "attributed" to the Tower in the book would be fictional, like King Kong on the Empire State Building, but his building would nevertheless be the actual building.) So the *fictional* Apex Tower cannot be found in any possible world. In this respect it is just like Dexter, the alligator. Properties like *being the Apex Tower* and *being Dexter* (the alligator) are *impossible* in just this sense, but notably *not* in any sense that implies that the properties themselves do not actually exist.

Now consider two tokens of the sentence, 'The Apex Tower does not exist'. One is actually uttered by someone to help dispel a confusion. The other is uttered by a deluded character in the book whose career was ruined by the success of the Apex project and who goes on to spend his time on the Bowery. According to my theory of names, the sentence has the form '$\neg\exists x$(x is-the-Apex-Tower)'. Intuitively, we want to think the token actually uttered is true, and the token in the story is false. To see whether this

[10] This sort of point has often been made by Saul Kripke.

can be maintained, we first ask whether the predicate expresses the same property in both occurrences.

I believe it does. This property, like all RSCs expressed by names, involves an actuality notion. I suggested above that that notion isn't *our* actuality notion, but is instead somehow relative to the world of the story. *Being the Apex Tower* is the property of *being a building that actually . . .*, with 'actually' understood in an appropriate story-relative way. Given such an understanding, it is clear how the two occurrences of the sentence can have different truth-values. It is simply a matter of their being evaluated in different "worlds." In the world of the story the property is instantiated; in the actual world it is not (even if the property *A is* instantiated).

I don't know how to elaborate the fictional actuality notion in detail. In effect this means I don't know how to elaborate the notion of the world of the story. But note that some obvious possibilities prove to be wrong. For example, the fictional 'actually' does *not* mean *according to this story*, for then the story would have to be seen as *asserting* that a building would be erected at a certain intersection, and so on. And this it clearly does not do. A more sophisticated attempt would be to take 'actually ' as a counterfactual qualification in the spirit of 'if this story were true, then. . . .'. But this isn't right either, for we have in effect already argued that the story could not be true at all if 'true' is taken seriously. And if it is instead just taken to express some weaker notion, like "fitting," then the story could "be true" with respect to intuitively different developers and buildings in different worlds. Of course then the property wouldn't be an RSC.

But it might be thought that no matter how the notion might be elaborated, I have already begged a question that should not be begged. Even if we accept the idea that fictional worlds are "incomplete," it might still be held that stories do not depict *specific* such incomplete worlds, but rather depict "world-types." For example, the world-type depicted by *The Apex Tower* would include lots of different worlds among which lots of intuitively different buildings would play the "Apex Tower role." This view would fit naturally with the rejected idea that stories are metaphysically possible, and that fictional worlds are fragments of metaphysically possible worlds. Though I have argued against this conception, the characterization I gave of fictional worlds is compatible with it. It would certainly be better not to beg this question. So let me try to answer it.

I think two considerations favor the specific-worlds view. First, it seems to me that if intuitively different buildings in different worlds have an equal claim to being depicted in *The Apex Tower*, then the story isn't really about a certain building. Instead it's about a certain building-type. Or better, it's about *any and every* building of a certain building-type. But it isn't. Stories are manifestly about specific people, buildings, and so forth. *The Apex Tower* is no exception. If it's true that nothing could be the Apex Tower, as I have held, then the story is about a certain impossible building, not about any building of a certain possible type. The second point is this. Imagine that two novelists quite independently happen to produce what is *lexically* the same (abstract) document. Have they written the same *novel*? The world-types account forces us to conclude that they have, but the specific-worlds account allows for the opposite conclusion – a conclusion that intuition strongly favors in a variety of cases.

Hence I hold that stories depict specific *impossible* worlds, and that they do not depict each and every world of a certain specific possible type. The worlds that stories depict are therefore not to be found among the possible worlds of typical metaphysical discourse (nor among fragments of such worlds). The fictional properties generated by stories, like *being the Apex Tower*, are impossible in the sense that they are necessarily uninstantiated. They – the properties – nevertheless exist, and this provides the basis for the (actual) truth of such statements as 'The Apex Tower does not exist'. The old adage that truth is stranger than fiction has things backwards. Fiction is much stranger since it is impossible even when it is perfectly consistent.

In Section 4, I urged that an occurrence of an ordinary proper name gets whatever existential force it has from the surrounding context (and not as part of the meaning of the name). I will conclude this section by suggesting how this idea fares in the case of fictional names. Consider a sentence like 'The Apex Tower is sixty stories tall'. Suppose it is (intuitively) true in the world of the story. Then we may assume that, in the world of the story, there is a general presupposition that the building exists. So occurrences of the sentence in the story will generally express a true proposition that has existential force. Of course there may be some contexts in the story in which the existential presupposition does not hold. For example, some characters may believe the building is fictional. For them the sentence will essentially have the form of a universally quantified subjunctive conditional, and so will express a proposition that has no existential force. (Whether it is true will depend on what they take to be the fictional details. This could prove to be rather tricky.)

The situation is exactly reversed in the actual world. Most of us know the building is fictional, and so make no existential presupposition in talking about it. When we say it is sixty stories tall we are in effect asserting a universal subjunctive conditional, and our assertion is true since the building was supposed to be that tall in the story. On the other hand, those among us who think the building actually exists do make the existential presupposition when they use the name. This mistake earns them an existential quantifier and a false belief.

5

Necessity and essentialism

The theory of names presented in Chapter 4 and some of the metaphysical doctrines that gave rise to it have various important modal features and consequences. Some of these have already been mentioned and some others may seem obvious or inevitable. In the present chapter I will try to sketch a general view about modality that fits well with the modal aspects of the views that have been advanced so far. This discussion will result in a new characterization of the doctrine of essentialism. Before proceeding to these matters we need to say more about *propositions* since the present view takes them to be the ultimate bearers of truth and hence of necessary and possible truth.

1. PROPOSITIONS

In Section 1.2 I assumed that propositions exist, and I have made free use of them since. Now it is time to consider them in greater detail. I will begin by saying what I think a genuinely "Platonist" commitment to propositions (and to any other sorts of "abstract" entities) involves. I think it involves something that has not always been noticed.[1] This discussion will be followed by a few remarks on how propositions are supposed to function.

I think *real* Platonism about abstract entities of any specific kind is a commitment to the existence of certain *specific* entities. This might seem pretty obvious, but there is a good reason for being explicit. It is that some philosophers think all that is needed for a genuine commitment to, say, natural numbers, is the belief that the

[1] Some of the views expressed here on what makes for genuine Platonism and what propositions must be like are discussed in Jubien (1989*b*, 1991).

axioms of the theory of numbers are "realized" in some domain *or other.* I think this is simply wrong. The axioms of the theory, suitably interpreted, might be *modeled*, say, in the domain of *celestial bodies*, or in the domain of *thoughts*. But *this* is a question about whether various quasi-mathematical objects exist, namely, certain impure sets, and it certainly has nothing to do with the question of the existence of *numbers*. But most philosophers who have thought about *realizations* of the axioms were thinking about something entirely different, something having nothing to do with sets. A person who believes the axioms are "realized" in this more "concrete" way believes there are objects that collectively display the characteristic structure associated with the theory. Such a person might truly be a Platonist, but so far only with respect to "the structure": He might believe there is a certain abstract *structure* that is actually instantiated or exemplified. But even if this belief were correct, it wouldn't follow that there are things in the world that are numbers.

But some philosophers think it does follow. They would say I have overlooked one of their premises. It is that numbers don't have any intrinsic features – that it is part of our very concept of a number that all of its properties are relational. After all, it is the essential properties of numbers that the theory concerns, and all of these properties are relational. (Also it is clear that the accidential properties of numbers are relational.) So it is claimed that all it takes for it to be true that there are numbers is that the structure be realized in some domain *or other.*

I have three comments. First, the premise is really a metaphysical howler. Any genuine existent has *some* intrinsic properties, if only the property of *being simple*. So to deny that numbers have intrinsic properties is in effect to deny that there are numbers! Such a denial should be accompanied by a nominalistic treatment of number talk. For example, the view that the theory is realized in the realm of the celestial bodies might support a version of nominalism about numbers.

This prompts the second comment. The rejected premise was offered in an effort to save the view that commitment to numbers only requires commitment to realization in some domain *or other.* But if the axioms were realized in *any* domain, say the celestial bodies, then they would be realized in a domain of objects that *do* have intrinsic properties. So the desired conclusion seems to falsify the premise that was invoked in trying to reach it.

To this it might be replied that no claim that (for example) the celestial bodies *are* the numbers was ever intended. The intended claim was merely that the existence of numbers – entities that have no intrinsic properties – depends only on there being *some* entities displaying the characteristic relational properties, even if those entities do have intrinsic properties. (Perhaps the motivating idea is that numbers are "abstract" in the sense of being "abstracted from" familiar objects – like celestial bodies – that display the right structure.)

But this is doubletalk. Our philosopher has given a *nominalistic* truth condition for the claim that numbers exist, but without realizing it is nominalistic. He says, in effect, that numbers exist if and only if there are objects that display the right structure, but then denies that these objects are the numbers. This is clearly a nominalistic reconstrual of an apparent (abstract) existence claim, since no abstract entities are asserted to exist in the given condition.

The third point is this. Our imagined philosopher is reasoning as if there really could be *realizations* of the structure of the numbers in, say, the physical world. Perhaps he would call them "concrete ω-realizations." But surely there could be no such things. Imagine, for example, that there were, at some specific time, denumerably many celestial bodies whose centers of mass were all located on the infinite line segment that begins at the center of mass of the sun and is determined by that same point and the center of mass of Mercury. Would *this* be a concrete ω-realization? Well, there could be no better candidate, but still it isn't good enough. What object in this infinite tableau would correspond to the number zero? The sun? Why? Zero has the relational property of not being greater than any natural number. But the *less-than* relation does *not* order the objects in the array. Of course there are indefinitely many type-ω orderings of the given objects, and the sun is the first element in many of them, but it is simply wrong to think that any of these well-orderings is induced by the *less-than* relation. For example, the relation *being closer to the sun than* induces an ordering in which the sun is first. But there are indefinitely many other relations that yield type-ω orderings that do not place the sun first. All of these are perfectly legitimate physical relations that the objects in the array bear to one another. The idea that the physical conglomeration itself somehow embodies a unique type-ω ordering of the celestial bodies is simply an illusion, and the idea that the objects "physically" exhibit the *less-than* relation is a fantasy fostered by that illusion.

Here is another example. Suppose someone who is *genuinely* committed to pure sets pins his "commitment" to *numbers* on the fact that the theory of numbers may be modeled among the sets. Then I would say that so far he is committed to sets, but *not yet* to natural numbers. Another philosopher might go further and claim that the numbers are not only modeled in a certain subrealm of the sets, but that each number is (literally) identical with a certain set in that realm. Then he *would* be committed to numbers (still assuming the commitment to sets was the genuine article). There would remain a serious problem, but not one that would threaten the genuineness of the commitment. The problem is the outlandishness of this view of the nature of numbers.

So I want to distinguish between commitments to *specific* entities and weaker "commitments" that may be understood some other way. I think it is only the former kind that are properly called *Platonism*. This is not to say that a commitment of a weaker variety may not *in some other way* be Platonist, as the first set-theoretic example illustrates. (The philosopher of that example is committed in a genuinely Platonist way to *sets*. But he is *not* committed in this way to *numbers*.) So when I speak of Platonism about, say, *numbers* or, more to our present interest, *propositions*, I have in mind a commitment to the existence of some *specific* entities that are held to be *numbers*, or *propositions*.

But what is it to be a *proposition* (or *number*, etc.)? We have seen, clearly I hope, that it is *not* to be an "entity having no intrinsic properties." The idea that there could be "intrinsically featureless" entities is an ontological absurdity. So if there really are propositions, then they *must* be entities that have intrinsic properties of one sort or another.

Now certainly it is possible to be ontologically committed to entities of a given kind without knowing anything very *precise* about their intrinsic natures. Many people have been committed to the existence of *stars* without knowing much about their internal natures. Yet they know there is *something* about their internal natures in which their being stars *consists*. They know that any star has the intrinsic property of *being a star*, but without knowing the ultimate analysis of that property.[2]

It is often claimed that we are "causally isolated" from abstract entities like numbers and propositions. *Perhaps* this is right. I won't take a stand. If it is right, it is surely of some importance. But suppose that we are so isolated. Then it seems to me that there are two important claims that notably do *not* follow from the isolation. First, it doesn't follow that there is no compelling argument in favor of the existence of such isolated entities as propositions. And second, it doesn't follow that we cannot know that such entities have certain sorts of intrinsic properties. The very most that might follow is that we cannot have detailed, analytical knowledge of their intrinsic properties. Our ultimate position is likely to be analogous to a layman's position with respect to the stars. He knows it is their intrinsic nature that makes them *stars*, makes them *glow*. And we know that the intrinsic nature of propositions makes them *propositions*, makes them . . . *represent*.

But how do we know this? How much do we know about the intrinsic properties of propositions? I characterized the notion of intrinsicalness in a rough way in Section 1.1, but was unable to offer a definition. Now, many pages later, I still have no definition. We will have to settle for the intuitive idea that a property of a thing is intrinsic if and only if it is a property that the thing has "in and of itself," and notably *not* in virtue of relations it bears to any things outside itself.

I have just argued that if there are any such entities as propositions, then they must have some intrinsic properties. Anyone who accepts propositions (along with an abundant realm of properties) will agree that there is a property of *being a proposition*. Of course it does not follow that the property of *being a proposition* is *intrinsic* to propositions. But I will now try to say why I think it is.

For a thing to be a proposition is clearly for it somehow *to represent*. The property of *being a proposition* seems in fact to be nothing

[2] Note that not all *kinds* are intrinsic properties. Although it is quite plausible to think that *being a star* is intrinsic, the same does not hold for *being a planet*. This does not, of course, mean that planets have no intrinsic natures. It merely means that the property of *being a planet* is relational. (In fact I would say it is a complex relational property with an intrinsic constituent. Roughly, it is to be a natural body of some significant size that orbits a star.)

but a certain sort of *representing*. For example, it is often said that a proposition "represents the world as being a certain way." Now, many things that are not propositions have a property of representing. A portrait represents its subject. A portrait of Catherine the Great has the property of *representing Catherine the Great*. But it doesn't have this property intrinsically. I would say, roughly, that it has the property in virtue of standing (or having stood) in one of a certain range of physical relations to Catherine, and so standing as a result of certain intentions of its painter (and probably Catherine's as well). This means it is a *relational* property: the projection obtained from a certain complex *relation* holding among the painting, Catherine, and the artist, by fixing the latter two *relata* as parameters. It *doesn't* have the property in and of itself, independently of the way Catherine and the painter are. Now it seems clear that propositions must either represent intrinsically, or else represent in something like the way portraits represent. But they *don't* represent in anything relevantly like the way portraits represent, as we shall now see.

Propositions are said to represent the world as being certain ways. For example, one of David Lewis's favorite propositions represents the world as containing a talking donkey. But its doing so does *not* depend in any way on what the world (or anything else) is like, and this is strikingly different from the case of the portrait. It isn't a matter of there being some *relation* holding between the proposition and the world in virtue of the way *they* are, and then *that* relation's being projected to a relational property by fixing the latter *relatum* as a parameter. The proposition represents that a donkey talks *regardless* of how the world or anything in it happens to be. I believe this ought to be the intuitive assessment of anyone who claims to accept *propositions*.

It is of course perfectly uncontroversial that the proposition *that a donkey talks* represents that a donkey talks, regardless of whether a donkey talks. But does it do so regardless of how *other* things stand in the world, say, regardless of how *we* stand? Well, propositions are supposed to be abstract entities that exist *independently* of us. So the proposition *that a donkey talks* represents that a donkey talks, regardless of whether a donkey talks, and *also* regardless of whether any speaker or believer stands in any particular relation to it. It would be truly absurd to think that even though the proposition does its representing regardless of how things stand with donkeys, and regardless of how things stand with us, there are nevertheless some *other* elements of the world that the representing is relationally dependent upon.[3] So we have no choice but to conclude that the representing is *not* a feature the proposition has for reasons at all like those that account for the portrait's representing Catherine. Thus the *representing* that propositions do can only be *intrinsic* to them. And thus the property of *being a proposition* is intrinsic to propositions.

The idea that propositions do their representing as part of their intrinsic natures may seem to be a "mystery." But according to the above argumentation it is an inevitable consequence of genuine Platonism about propositions (and properties). Some may see this as a powerful case against the Platonist account because they find the idea of intrinsic representation too mysterious to accept. But I think the case for propositional Platonism is so strong that we do better to try to get used to the mystery. I won't try to present that case in any detail. But its overall structure is this. Propositional Platonism is an essential ingredient of an impressively powerful account of language, thought, and communication. There is no rival account of these matters that dispenses with the propositions and is comparably powerful. In fact I think no rival account even comes close. Some future account may of course do the trick. If so, then I think (other things equal) it should prevail over the Platonist account. That merely means we should accept it as the superior account, but we should do so without overlooking the possibility that something even better may yet come along. It is exactly this attitude of provisional acceptance that I now hold concerning the Platonist account. (In fact I think this is the attitude we should have toward just about *any* theory we deem superior to its rivals.) So I think we should try to get used to the "mystery" of intrinsic representation. One way of doing this is to try to figure out just how mysterious it really is, and why. In fact I think it is not very mysterious at all, but it will take a little work to say why.

[3] Alvin Plantinga (1982) has revived the Augustinian idea that the representing is, in effect, dependent on a relation the proposition bears to God. But this strategy abandons genuine Platonism because the very existence of the proposition depends on God, and thus propositions are no longer independent of minds. It is only because this view abandons real Platonism that it escapes absurdity. The idea that there are independently existing *propositions* that do their *representing* only because they bear a certain relation to God really does seem absurd.

One of the puzzles of "intentionality" is this. How could a given thing "represent" or otherwise be "directed upon" something outside itself? There is a ready answer to this question, but it is an answer that produces another puzzle. A thing can be directed upon another thing as a result of *our* intentional activity. The painter's and Catherine's intentional activity brought it about that the painting represents her. The new puzzle is to say just how it is that they managed to bring this off. In other words, how does successful intentional activity work? In a way, this is not really a new puzzle, for any answer will surely depend on the painter's having his *own* representations of Catherine and of his painting (and it may depend on some of Catherine's representations as well). So any answer would, in effect, merely reduce the general problem of the outer-directedness of arbitrary things to the more specific case of the outer-directedness of minds. But certainly *this* problem is far from being solved. In fact it may be no exaggeration to call it a "mystery."

We are now at the edge of the mind–body problem, if not over the edge. If the reduction of the general problem of representation to the special case of mental representation is promising, then it must be because that a mind could represent is less of a mystery than that a relatively simple physical object like a painting could represent. Materialists find less mystery because the mind and its activity are dramatically more complex; dualists because the mind is a special thing of an entirely different sort. (Indeed some dualists have proposed intentionality as the characteristic emblem of the mental. This just means they thought it was an essential property, and that anything having it would thereby be "mental.")

Back to propositions: Our goal is to relieve the mystery of propositional representation, or at least make it seem a more respectable mystery. Notice that the strategy of reducing the problem to the case of what we *normally* think of as "the mental" is unavailable since propositions do their representing intrinsically. But the general thrust of that strategy was that representation by an intuitively incompetent entity was dissolved into representation by an intuitively more competent entity. That more-competent entity was more competent either because of extra complexity or because it was an entity of an entirely different, special kind – nothing like the incompetent entity. But evidently both of these characterizations also apply to propositions.

Certainly propositions must be complex entities in order to represent intrinsically. There is no reason to suppose that they are not, in fact, amazingly complex, more complex than the portrait of Catherine, perhaps more complex than the human brain. They are also entities of a very special kind, markedly different from the portrait. Thus the most general claim that a materialist could make in pressing the reductive strategy *and* the most general claim that a dualist could make to the same end, are *both* available for *nonreductive* deployment in favor of propositions.

But still it might be held that representation is necessarily a *conscious* phenomenon, and that the "representing" that the painting does is called such only by a courtesy – that it is entirely derivative from conscious representation. And, of course, it is absurd to think that strictly abstract entities are capable of consciousness.

But do we really know that representation *must* be conscious? I suppose that if we take certain Freudian claims as purely metaphorical (or else reject them), then it certainly seems that *our* (nonderivative) representing is always conscious. But it would be sheer parochialism to conclude that all representation is *necessarily* conscious. It would be wrong to infer this even if we did know how our own representing works.

But surely we *don't* know this. It is worth noting that the likely *relational* character of our representing does nothing to dispel the mystery. We can imagine all sorts of relations that might hold between mental configurations and things outside – various sorts of matchings, isomorphisms, and what not. What we find is a variety of candidates that are intuitively well suited to represent – they have a promising "structure." But we still don't understand how they manage to do it, because it is perfectly clear that the matching, isomorphism, or whatever is insufficient. Some crucial element is still missing. We haven't managed to capture the "intentionality." (To say that we adopt a private *convention* that the mental configuration represents the outside thing of course does not help. We could not adopt such a convention without a prior representation of the outside thing.) So our own presumably *relational* representing remains a mystery, but it's one we don't hesitate to accept.

I think the *intrinsic* representing that propositions are supposed to do is actually less mysterious than our own representing. As we have just been discussing, the central problem with our representing – the one that just won't go away – is its outer-directedness. So it may at first seem doubly mysterious that a *proposition* could represent: for one thing, it must achieve outer-directedness, which is already bad enough, but on top of this, it must do so *intrinsically.*

The mind may reel at such a double mystery. But it shouldn't, because the mystery rests on a mistake: the assumption that propositional representation is outer directed. If it were, then it would indeed suffer whatever problems attend outer-directedness in its other manifestations. But I will now try to develop a case that propositional representation is not outer directed at all. The idea that it *is* outer directed is encouraged by the picture of propositions "representing *the world* as being certain *ways.*" Certainly *the world* is something at least partly outside any proposition. And perhaps *ways* are outside too. But let's look more closely.

The proposition *that a donkey talks* is supposed to represent *the world* as being a certain way, as containing a talking donkey. We are quite used to hearing this, but something is fishy. Consider the proposition *that Fido is a dog*. It is very natural to say it represents Fido as being a dog. So *maybe* it should somehow "represent" that particular dog and that particular property, entities that may be outside it. (For the merest moment, let's not worry about the Fallacy of Reference.) But it seems bizarre to say that it must also represent *the world*. If we want a natural candidate for representing *the world*, there is a closely related proposition that stands a much better chance: the proposition *that the world is such that Fido is a dog*. This proposition is distinct from the (necessarily equivalent) proposition *that Fido is a dog*. Similarly, the proposition *that the world contains a talking donkey* is distinct from the proposition *that a donkey talks*. The fact that they are necessarily equivalent of course means it is usually harmless to say that the latter proposition represents the world as containing a talking donkey. The point, however, is that this is literally false if we are being careful about our representation talk. Intuitively speaking, the world is not a "constituent" of the proposition *that a donkey talks*, but it is a constituent of the proposition *that the world contains a talking donkey*. So such a proposition *might* legitimately be said to represent the world. But the former proposition could at most be said to represent *part* of the world. (Of course there is a loose sense in which representing part of the world would count as representing the world.)

But just how might a proposition represent either the world *or* part of it as being a certain way? Suppose the proposition *that there is a dog in the yard* is true. Then there is some "concrete situation" – a chunk of the physical world containing the relevant yard and some dog – that the proposition might at first be thought to represent. And any chunk of the physical world would certainly seem to be something outside the abstract proposition. But it simply cannot be right that this is what the proposition represents.

For one thing, that chunk of the world has features that the proposition says nothing at all about. If the dog happens to be black, then the proposition *that there is a black dog in the yard* would have to represent precisely the same thing as the original proposition. But of course it doesn't. Further, what if the original proposition were false? Would it then represent what would be a *different* concrete situation – a chunk including a certain dog-bereft yard (or no one yard)? Not at all. What a proposition represents does *not* depend on its truth-value. After all, its representing is supposed to be intrinsic, but its truth-value isn't. The fact that it *is* (generally) parts of the world that *make* propositions true or false can easily mislead us into thinking that propositions *represent* parts of the world. But I hope we now see that this cannot really be right.

There is no real alternative but to conclude that propositions (at least *some* propositions) represent specific properties (or relations) as being (or not being) variously instantiated. Then they are made to be true or false according to whether parts of the world do the appropriate instantiating. Thus consider again the proposition *that there is a dog in the yard*. It represents the properties *being a dog* and *being in the yard* as standing in the relation of *being jointly instantiated* (that is, the relation that one property bears to another if and only if at least one thing instantiates them both).

The proposition *that Fido is a dog* represents the properties *being Fido* and *being a dog* as standing in the relation of *being jointly instantiated*. (Here we refuse to commit the Fallacy of Reference.) And the proposition *that a donkey talks* represents the properties *being a donkey* and *talking* as standing in the relation of *being jointly instantiated*. (Note that the proposition *that there is a talking donkey* merely represents the property of *being a talking donkey* as having the property of *being instantiated*. Of course these two propositions are necessarily equivalent.)

Perhaps the *only* representing that propositions *ever* do is representing that various properties and relations are (or are not) variously instantiated. Although I have no general theory to offer at this time, I believe this is correct. In conformity with such a theory, propositions could legitimately be seen as "representing" the (concrete) world (or parts of the world) only *derivatively*, strictly in virtue of the fact that their truth-values depend on how things are in the world or in parts of the world.

But how might a proposition represent a given property as being instantiated? We have long since concluded that it must somehow do it *intrinsically*. This now means that the proposition must contain elements that intrinsically represent the relevant property and the relation of instantiation. But there could be no better representative of a property or relation than that very property or relation *itself*. In fact it is the only candidate that could conceivably make the representing *intrinsic*. So I conclude that propositions must be entities that prominently include properties and relations as "constituents." But I have no view on the exact nature of the constituency relation.

It could be that propositions are certain mereological sums, sums that include properties and relations as parts (perhaps along with certain other elements).[4] Then the constituency relation would simply be (a restriction of) the *part–whole* relation. A purely mereological account would have a number of hurdles to clear, notably those reflecting the familiar *theoretical* weakness of mereology as compared to, say, set theory. But I am not convinced it is unattainable.

Naturally there are other possibilities. But it is important to see that it doesn't really matter what the exact intrinsic nature of constituency happens to be. If we are causally isolated from propositions in some serious way, then we will never be able to find out. What does matter is that we have been able to reach *some* conclusions about the intrinsic natures of propositions *without* investigating them directly. It shouldn't be surprising that the conclusions we have reached could be *realized* in different ways. Even if we were able to give a perfectly smooth and seductive mereological account, we would not thereby have established that propositions actually *are* those mereological sums, and hence that constituency is part–whole. So it may be that constituency will forever remain at least somewhat dark, and thus propositions will always have an element

[4] Some philosophers may balk at the idea of "extending" mereology into the realm of the abstract. They may think it is somehow essentially confined to the realm of the spatiotemporal. I think this is profoundly wrong, but I won't discuss it here. Lewis (1991) discusses and rejects the idea that mereology is restricted to the spatiotemporal, and goes on to develop the mereology of *classes*.

of mystery. But it is a mystery we should be able to live with if it is just our isolation that makes it impossible to unravel.

It is worth emphasizing that the mystery concerns the exact nature of constituency, but *not* the fact that constituency occurs. If there really are propositions, then it *must* occur, one way or another, just as intrinsic representation must occur. It also must be that properties and relations (including instantiation) *are* constituents of propositions. We are finally able to see clearly that propositional representation is not outer directed. Propositions represent of properties and relations that they are variously instantiated (or uninstantiated). The representing they do is therefore of their own constituents. Since the representing is intrinsic, constituency *must* be *some* sort of part–whole relation, possibly the part–whole relation of mereology. So propositional representation is not outer directed. In this crucial respect it is dramatically *less* mysterious than the representing that is done by us, even though we do not know the exact nature of constituency. So I think the score is Propositional Representation 1, Mental Representation 0.

But this may not be the final score. For there is something else that is a bit mysterious about propositional representation. Take the proposition *that there are dogs*. It represents the property *being a dog* as having the property *being instantiated*. So it has these two constituents. But how does it link them *propositionally*? One way to see the force of this question is to imagine that propositions really are mereological sums. Then the two properties are parts of the proposition. But the proposition must have some further parts, for otherwise there would be no reason to see it as representing that being a dog is instantiated. It could equally well be seen as representing that instantiation is a dog, or that there are dogs and instantiations. In fact there is no reason to see the sum of the two properties as representing that *anything* is the case, despite its having parts that are admirable representations of the two properties. So the proposition (whether a mereological sum or not) would need some further part or parts to link the properties propositionally and to do so in the right way. The exact nature of this further propositional ingredient is no clearer to us than is that of constituency. But, as with constituency, we already know enough to conclude that it *must* be there and must do precisely this job. Otherwise it cannot be a *proposition*. If we are in fact causally isolated, then we will probably never know much more about its intrinsic nature.

It might be thought that mental representation evens the score here, for we can supply the needed propositional component by an intentional act. This has a soothing ring, perhaps because we sometimes experience intentional *feelings*, but the fact remains that we do not understand how our intentional activity works in the first place. We just believe it does. If one day we should come to understand this, and our understanding yields a plausible account of the endowing of representations with propositional force, then I think a point would indeed have been made and the score perhaps tied. But as of now I think we have a standoff on the question of propositional force. In both cases we think something is going on, and in both cases we don't know exactly how it works. So right now the overall score remains 1–0. This score merely reflects the conviction that there is one vital respect in which propositional representation seems less mysterious than mental representation – and that in other respects they seem about equally mysterious. (I don't mean to suggest that we face a question of choosing between the two. I think *both* sorts of representation take place, and indeed that our own propositional representation consists in our standing in a certain relation to a *proposition*!)

I will conclude this section by making explicit a few assumptions about how propositions function in the somewhat larger picture. First, I am assuming that it is propositions that are the fundamental bearers of truth-values, not sentences or sentence-tokens. This means that if it is ever appropriate to say of an entity other than a proposition that it is *true* (or *false*), then it is so *derivatively* (as a reflection of the truth of some specific proposition). I am also assuming that every proposition is either true or false.

Not every *declarative sentence* has a truth-value. For example, 'I'm hungry' has no truth-value. It has no truth-value because it is not definitively and uniquely associated with a single specific proposition. So there is no natural source from which it might derive a truth-value. On the other hand, genuine *tokens* of 'I'm hungry' normally do have truth-values. (I won't worry about apparent tokens in plays, on hypnotist's couches, in states of delirium, and so on.) When a token has a truth-value, it does so because it *expresses* (or perhaps *asserts*, but at least figures in the *assertion of*) a proposition. Then it has whatever truth-value the proposition it expresses (or asserts, etc.) has. There may be some declarative sentences *any* genuine token of which would express the same proposition. ('Dogs are mammals' (in English), for example?) Such sentences may be thought of as having doubly derivative truth-values in the obvious way. I take it that sentences are themselves abstract entities, and that sentence-tokens generally are not. It is probably best to think of sentences as certain complex properties, properties that could be instantiated by something if and only if it was a token of that sentence. (So *tokening* would just be *instantiation* restricted to a co-domain consisting of the sentences.) It is worth noting that something with all the configurational earmarks of a token of a certain sentence clearly need not be such. It might have come to have that configuration by sheer physical accident. Therefore a certain intentional element seems required. (A consequence is that if sentences *are* properties of the sort suggested, then they are not purely configurational properties.)

So I have assumed that propositions are the fundamental bearers of truth and falsity. I will also assume that *necessity* and *possibility* are "modes" of truth (and falsity). So it will be propositions that are the fundamental bearers of *necessary* (and *possible*) *truth* (and *falsity*).

2. PROPERTY ENTAILMENT

Being red entails *having a color. Being a sister* entails *being female*. It is natural to try to explain the relation of entailment between properies by saying that a property *P entails* a property Q just in case it is necessary that anything that has *P* also has Q.[5] But I think just the reverse is appropriate: What makes it necessary that anything having *P* also has Q is the fact that a certain relation holds between the properties *P* and Q, a relation we may as well call *entailment*. (This notion of entailment can be extended to the realm of *relations*, generating a parallel connection with the notion of necessity. I will not discuss entailment between relations in any detail in what follows.)

I think this should be the position of anyone who is really a *Platonist* about properties. Let me try to say why. As with *propositions* and *numbers*, genuine Platonism about *properties* is the view that there exist certain entities that have a certain *intrinsic* property – in this case, the property of *being a property*. But what is this property? Roughly, it is *admitting of instantiation*. This does not mean that a property *must* be instantiated. It means that a property is an entity

[5] In fact I did just this (with my fingers crossed) in Section 3.1.

whose internal nature *allows* it to be instantiated if things in the world will only cooperate. Platonists believe that properties somehow *make things be the ways they are*. This "making" is not generally thought to be *causal* in nature. Nor is it in any useful way *explanatory*. Rather it is *constitutive*. A thing's instantiating redness just constitutes its being red. The instantiation of properties is undoubtedly as mysterious as the representation that is done by propositions. I will not make an effort to soften the present mystery as I did in the case of propositions. By now it should be clear that my overall view is that if you really accept these entities, then you should accept them in their full, if somewhat mysterious, glory. The alternative is to convert to nominalism.

So, if instantiating properties is what makes things be the way they are, then it *must* be that the properties have some complex intrinsic nature that contributes to the overall way-making enterprise. In other words, instantiation is a relation between a thing and a property that depends on the intrinsic nature of the property. Of course it may depend on other things as well; for example, on the intrinsic nature of the thing, and even on relations the thing bears to other things. But the key point is that a thing's being, say, *red*, must depend (in part) on the way *redness* itself is.

So suppose *being red* has a certain intrinsic feature *R* that accounts for its making things be a certain characteristic way, and suppose *being colored* has a similar feature *C* that plays a similar role. Then there must be a certain *intrinsic* relation holding between the two *properties* that supervenes on the features *R* and *C*. The exact nature of this relation, say *E*, depends entirely on the exact natures of *R* and *C*. If we really are causally isolated from properties, then we won't be able to find out more about *E* by inspecting it or by inspecting *R* and *C*. But whatever its exact nature may be, *E* is what lies behind the fact that things that are made to be a certain way by instantiating *being red* are *thereby* made to be the very way things are made to be by instantiating *being colored*. *E* is of course the relation of *entailment* (*between properties*).

Thus it seems to me that genuine Platonism about properties is committed to the existence of an intrinsic relation of entailment between properties. Because this relation supervenes on the way-making characteristics of the properties it links, it is the real source of the *necessity* in propositions expressed by sentences like 'Necessarily, whatever is red is colored' and 'Necessarily, all sisters are female'.

Suppose it is necessary that anything having property *P* also has property Q. Suppose also that *P* and *Q* really exist independently of minds, languages, and the like. It might have been thought that there is nothing about the natures of *P* and *Q* that accounts for the necessity. In fact it might have been thought that nothing "accounts" for it at all, that necessity is just a simple, unanalyzable property that some true propositions have and all other propositions lack. It's just the way things are (or, actually, have to be). (A variation would be that God simply dictates which truths are necessary.) I hope the above considerations show that this view, though perhaps coherent, does not mesh well with real Platonism about properties. It is a view that could only appeal to someone not fully aware of the real nature of Platonism.

A different view is that what accounts for the necessity of the proposition is just that it is true in all possible worlds, and that by consulting our intuitions about possible worlds we can often come to reasonable conclusions about what's necessary and what isn't. I think this is simply an evasion. No account of the ontological nature of possible worlds settles *by itself* whether there are worlds in which some red thing is not colored. All the weight is carried by modal intuition. The intuition that "there is no possible world in which a red thing is not colored" is just a colorful version of the intuition that it's necessary that red things are colored. It's an intuition of a necessity that is in no way *accounted for* by the Goldbergian apparatus of the worlds.[6] The rejected view that necessity is a simple, unanalyzable property is actually less of an evasion, since it could be accompanied by the claim that we have generally reliable intuitions about whether a given truth enjoys the property.

I will not consider other attempts to ground entailment in a prior notion of necessity. It seems to me that no matter how they might go, they must inevitably seem less plausible than grounding necessity in entailment, given that they retain genuine Platonism about properties. The reason is simply that they are committed to the way-making features of properties, but then ignore them in grounding the notion of entailment.

I will conclude this section by suggesting what I think is a compelling conception of how entailment might work. This conception makes vivid how it is that entailment could be an intrinsic relation.

[6] A number of criticisms of possible worlds are given in Jubien (1988).

Suppose properties have other properties as *mereological parts*. Perhaps *being colored* is part of *being red*, *being female* is part of *being a sister*, and *being a dog* is part of *being Fido*. To say that *P* entails Q then might merely mean that Q is a part of *P*. Property entailment might be the *whole–part* relation (restricted to the realm of properties). Then *instantiation* would be a "distributive" relation – one that holds between an arbitrary thing and an arbitrary property only if it holds between that thing and all of the parts of that property. This mereological account would give us what we're looking for. Since something instantiates *P* only if it instantiates every part of *P*, and *Q* is a part of *P*, it is necessary that if a thing instantiates *P*, it also instantiates *Q*.

Thus I believe there is a way of conceiving properties that makes it easy to see how certain very natural relations between them could have the sort of logical effects the entailment view is committed to. But now note the following. We are assuming that properties exist. So they *must* have a certain mereology, even if it is the trivial mereology in which no property is a part of any property other than itself. But it is in fact very plausible to think that it isn't the trivial mereology. According to genuine Platonism, it is the properties that a thing has that make it *how it is*. Suppose a thing is *red* and *colored*. These are distinct properties. But it is impossible to deny that anything instantiating the first must instantiate the second. It is hard to overlook the idea that the way the thing is in virtue of *being red* somehow "includes" the way it is in virtue of *being colored*. If *being red* makes a thing be a way that includes the way things are made to be by *being colored*, then we have a neat explanation of the intuitive necessity. But how could *being red* have this extra power? The most natural answer is that it isn't *extra* at all. It has the power because *being colored* is *part* of it, and instantiation distributes over parts.

I think of the mereological account as an innocent hypothesis about the nature of properties. There are a number of difficult questions a full development of the idea would have to face, and I certainly don't know the answers to all of them.[7] Furthermore, there may be no way for us to know that it's actually true because

[7] For example, is there a good reason to believe the mereology of properties makes a property like *being red or round* a part of *being red*, but not *vice versa*, independently of our intuitions about entailment?

we may be isolated from properties in some important way. But the hypothesis has a certain heuristic value even if it isn't true, because something *like* it must be true. There must be *some* intrinsic relation that holds between properties and accounts for property entailment.

3. NECESSITY *DE DICTO*

It is convenient to introduce the *de dicto/de re* distinction with respect to *sentences* rather than *propositions*. This is because it is a relatively easy matter to ground the distinction in the scopes of "modal operators" in sentences. (There is a problem with this procedure in the case of ordinary language, because most speakers probably use sentences with contrasting placements of the modal adverbs interchangeably, and aren't sensitive to the distinction in any guise.) Our position is that propositions are the fundamental truth bearers, and that necessity is a "mode" of truth. Accordingly, it must be propositions that are the entities fundamentally susceptible of necessity, that is, of necessary truth. So, even if it is often useful to think of the distinction as linguistically drawn, it is nevertheless to propositions that it fundamentally applies.

I think that the phenomenon that is commonly called necessity *de dicto* is entirely explained by entailment relations among properties (and relations and logic). Let us consider this claim with the help of a few examples. We will ask what propositions the following sentences express.

(1) 'Necessarily, all dogs are mammals.' Taken *de dicto,* it means that the proposition *that all dogs are mammals* is necessarily true. That is, sentence (1) expresses the proposition *that (the proposition that) all dogs are mammals is necessarily true.* So it asserts of a certain proposition that it is necessarily true. It asserts this of the proposition *that all dogs are mammals.* Now, what makes this nonmodal proposition *true* is that everything with the property of *being a dog* also has the property of *being a mammal.* What makes it *necessarily* true is that the property of *being a dog* in fact *entails* the property of *being a mammal.* This is my view. In contrast, on a routine possible-worlds account, the necessity would be grounded somehow or other in the (claimed) fact that the proposition *that all dogs are mammals* is true in every possible world.

(2) 'Necessarily, seven is prime.' Here the *de dicto/de re* distinction is sometimes thought to be a distinction without a difference. It is thought that the sentences (2) and (2*) 'Seven is necessarily prime', express the same proposition. Here is a possible-worlds account of why this might be

thought. The proposition expressed by (2) is true iff the proposition *that seven is prime* is true in every possible world. The proposition expressed by (2*) is true iff the entity *seven* has the property *being necessarily prime*. But seven has *this* property iff it has the property *being prime* in every world. That is, iff the proposition *that seven is prime* is true in every world.

There are several reasons why this is not a good argument. First, it would at best show that the propositions expressed by (2) and (2*) are necessarily equivalent, not that they are identical, since 'iff' merely expresses material equivalence. A related problem is that it assumes that to have the property *being necessarily prime* is simply to have the property *being prime* in every world. But on some views of "necessary properties" these phenomena might be distinct (even if necessarily equivalent).

Of greater importance to our present concerns is that the argument in effect assumes that 'seven' is a rigid designator. If it isn't, then finding out whether the proposition *that seven is prime* is true in every world isn't relevant to the question whether the entity *seven* is necessarily prime. Now, I do not want to maintain that 'seven' isn't a rigid designator. (In Section 4.6 I claimed that the names of abstract entities *are* plausibly held to be rigid designators.) My point is simply to make the assumption explicit, because a similar assumption will surface in the case to be considered next. For now I conclude from the above discussion that it isn't automatically true that the sentences (2) and (2*) express the same proposition. Whether they do depends on a variety of questions that may be answered in different ways by different theories.

(3) 'Necessarily, Cicero is human.' Here matters are relevantly as they were in case (2), but for the complication that although seven is (presumably) a necessary existent, Cicero is not. We will deal with this complication in a moment. On any possible-worlds account, (3) expresses a true proposition iff in each of a certain class of worlds, the proposition *that Cicero is human* is true. We have seen, in effect, that it is not automatic that this is the condition that must be met in order to make it true that *Cicero* is necessarily human (on that same account). So there is familiar room in possible-worlds accounts for the view that the *de dicto* and the *de re* are different propositions. We will see below that on the present theory of proper names, they are very different indeed. The *de dicto* proposition expressed by (3) is true on a worlds account because the proposition *that Cicero is human* is true in every (relevant) world. It is true on my account because the property of *being Cicero* entails the property of *being human*.

Let us consider this claim in a little more detail. On the present theory of names, 'Cicero is human' may be translated into the explicitly quantificational sentence

$$\exists x(x \text{ is-Cicero} \ \& \ x \text{ is human}).$$

Certainly *this* does not express a necessarily true proposition. The problem, of course, is the existential import. So if (3) itself is to be true, it must receive a reading that makes a suitable adjustment for the possibility that Cicero does not exist. In world theory the adjustment is, roughly, either abandoning existential import by allowing that the proposition that Cicero is human may be true in worlds where Cicero doesn't exist, or else evaluating the claim of necessity only with respect to worlds where Cicero does exist.

As I emphasized in Chapter 4, I think most ordinary uses of ordinary proper names *do* have existential force, and the presence of the modal adverb in (3) does nothing to diminish it. We therefore seek a reading that is committed to Cicero's existence but conditionalizes on his existence in the strictly modal part of the claim. This is not hard to find. We take the sentence 'Necessarily, Cicero is human' to mean *Cicero exists, and necessarily, if Cicero exists, then he is human*, and translate it by

$$\exists x(x \text{ is-Cicero}) \,\&\, \Box\forall y(y \text{ is-Cicero} \supset y \text{ is human}).$$

But the universal conditional that lies in the scope of the modal operator *must* express a true proposition because the property of *being Cicero* entails the property of *being human*. Thus we see that the *de dicto* part of the claim expressed by (3) is true strictly in virtue of the entailment of one property by another.

I cannot think of a plausible *de dicto* necessity that isn't relevantly like either case (1) or case (3). Thus it seems to me that the phenomenon of necessity *de dicto* rests entirely on entailment relations among properties (and relations), and logic. Of course there certainly are cases that display more logical complexity than (1) and (3). In such cases necessities may rely on logic and on "intermediate" entailments that aren't explicitly present in the sentence in question. Here is a relatively simple example: 'Necessarily, if there is a husband, there is a wife.' With explicit quantifiers:

$$\Box\forall x[x \text{ is a husband} \supset \exists y(y \text{ is a wife})].$$

This necessary truth depends on an intermediate entailment. *Being a husband* entails *having a wife*, that is, *being such that there is a wife that one has*. So anything instantiating the former property must instantiate the latter. But if the latter property is instantiated, then the proposition *that there is a wife* follows by logic.

A general theory that grounds all *de dicto* necessity in entailment and logic is beyond the scope of this book. It would obviously require a good deal of effort to produce such a theory. (For one thing it seems to presuppose a general theory of properties.) But I believe the claim that *de dicto* necessity is so grounded has been made plausible even without the theory.

In the above discussion I have avoided the term 'analytic'. To be *analytic* is to be true "in virtue of the meanings of terms." Propositions (and judgments, etc.) don't *have* terms. So it must be *sentences* to which the notion of analyticity applies first and foremost.

(Of course, it might be useful to extend the notion so that it applies derivatively to propositions.) Then how does the notion of analyticity fit with what I have been claiming about necessity *de dicto*? I have claimed that a proposition is necessary (*de dicto*) if and only if it is true in virtue of property (and relation) entailments (and logic). Now properties are quite plausibly thought of as the *meanings* of predicates (including, of course, *disguised* predicates). So the way is clear for the view that a sentence is analytic if and only if it expresses a proposition that is necessary *de dicto*. I won't try to solidify this connection.

4. NECESSITY *DE RE*

"Essentialist" philosophers believe such things as *that Cicero is necessarily human*. This proposition seemingly asserts "of Cicero" that he has a certain modal property, the property of *being necessarily human*. It is therefore thought to be a typical example of a true attribution of a necessary property to a specific thing.

But I think this is wrong. It will be easier to say why if we assume a materialist view of persons. (This is harmless since we could have picked an uncontroversially physical example.) It seems to me that if the '*re*' in 'necessity *de re*' is taken seriously, then there is only one plausible way to understand 'Cicero is necessarily human' as expressing a *de re* necessity about the thing "Cicero." On this understanding, 'Cicero' is taken – somehow or other – to pick out a certain *specific physical object*, and that object is asserted to be necessarily human. But it also seems to me that on this understanding the proposition expressed is clearly false. Let me explain.

If 'Cicero' picks out a certain specific physical object, then it must pick out a certain mereological sum of physical stuff. According to our ontological naturalism, *there simply are no physical objects that are not mereological sums of physical stuff. To be a physical object is nothing more nor less than to be such a mereological sum*. In the ontology of **M+**, to be such is to be the material content of some specific region of space-time. (In a more physically sophisticated ontology, we might have to settle for something a little less definite, something with probabilities somehow involved or whatever; no matter – nothing will depend on the difference.) So now we have to ask whether this *thing* (*res*) is necessarily human. Surely it is actually human. But I don't see how it could be necessarily human since it is clearly possible that its parts be arranged in such a way that it isn't human at all. Surely there are worlds in which that very thing exists, but is a widely scattered object. Surely there are also worlds in which it isn't a widely scattered object, but its parts are assembled so that it isn't an animal of any sort, isn't even a living thing. It is very easy to imagine the same stuff existing but not even coming close to having the property of *being human*. So I think that on the present understanding of the *de re*, the proposition is plainly false.

It is worth emphasizing that it is this understanding that the *usual* notion of the *de re* incorporates: the attribution of a modal property *to a specific thing* – if you like, some entity treated in the ontology of **M+**; if you don't like, some other, irrelevantly different entity. But note that very different semantical theories are capable of achieving the *de re* in this sense. An obvious example is the theory that takes 'Cicero' as *directly referring* to a specific physical thing. Another example is provided by the theory of names I am advocating in this book. According to that theory, and including the required dose of existential charity, 'Cicero is necessarily human' may be translated by

$$\exists x[x \text{ is-Cicero} \;\&\; \Box(\exists y(y = x) \supset x \text{ is human})].$$

Of course this sentence expresses a *false* proposition, just as any standardly *de re* formulation *must*, for the reason given above.

I don't think there is anything special about this case. I believe that all of the usual examples of *de re* necessities offered by essentialists collapse under possible rearrangements of parts. Briefly, consider the well-known case of Kripke's *table* (or, sometimes, *lectern*). Is *it* necessarily made of wood? Certainly not. Clearly it could be rearranged even at the molecular level so that it wasn't made of wood. We could have that very thing, perhaps widely scattered, perhaps not, and not have something that was made of wood at all. I will return to the case of the table a little later. There I will consider a *de re* claim about it that might be thought to survive the present sort of criticism, even if the claim that it is necessarily made of wood does not.

Despite all of this, it may still be felt that there must be *some* truth in the intuition that Cicero is necessarily human and the table is necessarily made of wood, even if *de re* formulations fail to capture it. Indeed I think there is, but I will postpone discussing the matter until the next section.

Not all cases of apparent modality *de re* are expressed by sentences containing proper names. Consider the sentence 'Any house could have lacked some of its parts'. We would normally think it expresses a true proposition, but consider the first explicitly *de re* formulation that is likely to come to mind:

$$\forall x[x \text{ is a house} \supset \exists y(Pyx \mathbin{\&} \neg\Box Pyx)].$$

This sentence is *false* because every thing has its parts essentially, including things that happen to be houses. So it doesn't capture the sense in which the original sentence is intuitively true. That sentence is true because no matter what house we pick, it has at least one dispensable part. But this means that some thing could have counted intuitively as *the same house* while lacking such a part. This strongly suggests that the original proposition involves an implicit quantification over certain *properties*. Now, for every house, there is the property of *being that house* (on analogy with property P of Section 3.4 and property H of 4.4). Call any such property a *house-property* (similarly for any other category: dog, celestial body, globe, and so forth). Now we may translate as follows:

$$\forall x(x \text{ is a house} \supset \exists H\{H \text{ is a house-property} \\ \mathbin{\&} x \text{ has } H \mathbin{\&} \exists y[Pyx \mathbin{\&} \neg\Box\forall z(z \text{ has } H \supset Pyz)]\}).$$

The proposition this sentence expresses is true. Moreover, it captures the intuitive content of the original sentence, but without being *de re* with respect to x, the variable that ranges over the things that are the houses. It is, of course, *de re* with respect to both H (an abstract entity) and y (a mereological sum featured in a part–whole assertion). So it is a true proposition involving modality *de re*, but not the modality *de re* it was originally thought to involve. It is not the sort of *de re* talk that raises any problems of the sort considered above. Sometimes talk about a house is merely talk about a mereological sum, but when the talk gets *modal*, it is generally covert *de re* talk about the house-property the mereological sum instantiates. (It is beyond the scope of this book to discuss this phenomenon in detail.)

5. THE ESSENSE OF ESSENTIALISM

I have tried to defend the principle of mereological essentialism, and I have explicitly embraced certain *de re* necessities. For example, if 'α' and 'β' are rigid designators of two mereological sums (as contemplated in Section 4.6), and α is a part of β, then I think the proposition expressed by 'β necessarily has part α' is a true *de re* necessity. It asserts truly *of* a specific mereological sum that *it* has a certain property – the property of being related in a certain necessary way to a certain other specific mereological sum. We saw a more complicated example in the house case just considered in Section 4. But of course "mereological" cases like these are a far cry from the sort of example usually advanced in favor of "essentialism." As we have seen, I think those examples are generally doomed to fail because of possible rearrangements of parts.

So it may look like I ought to think the only genuine essentialism in the physical realm is *mereological* essentialism. In fact I once thought this, but I don't anymore. The reason is that I now think it is wrong to characterize essentialism in the way we are accustomed, in terms of necessary properties of *things*. As long as they are properly understood, I agree with the essentialist's intuitions about, say, Cicero or Kripke's table. Moreover, I think these intuitions support a genuine and nontrivial thesis of *essentialism*.

The real opponent of essentialism is *not* the philosopher who says that no mereological sum is necessarily human or necessarily made of wood. These claims are so hard to deny that they ought to be compatible with the essentialist's intuitions. It isn't plausible that essentialism is wrong for such obvious reasons. The real opponent of essentialism is the person who – one way or another – claims there are worlds in which, say, Cicero is a cat or Kripke's table is made of plastic. But the philosopher who propounds these possibilities does not typically see himself as making obvious assertions about specific mereological sums, nor need he be. There must be some way of understanding the debate over essentialism that doesn't make the anti-essentialist such an easy winner.

So I think there are two fundamentally different ways to understand the claim that, say, Cicero could not have been a cat. One *is* as a *de re* assertion about a mereological sum. This assertion is easily – I have said *too* easily – seen to be false. But the other takes it as a *de dicto* assertion whose truth hinges on the incompatibility of two specific properties. I think the *real* debate over essentialism concerns *this* sort of assertion rather than the former. Let me elaborate.

Imagine the following exchange between two metaphysicians. One says, "*Being Cicero* is incompatible with *being a cat*. In any world where you find *Cicero*, you find something that *is not a cat*. Nothing could have both properties." And so on. Then the other disagrees. It seems to me that these people are arguing about *essentialism*, and I think the "essentialist" view that the properties are incompatible is right. Furthermore, I think it is captured perfectly in the *de dicto* claim that it is necessary that anything that has the property *being Cicero* has the property of *not being a cat*. That is, it is captured perfectly by:

$$\Box\forall x(x \text{ is-Cicero} \supset x \text{ is not a cat}).$$

The tendency to overlook this in favor of a standard *de re* formulation about a specific *thing* is obviously rooted in the Fallacy of Reference. But the debate over essentialism isn't really a debate about reference. What the essentialist is really after, I think, is simply the *general*, *unanalyzed* intuition that (say) *Cicero couldn't be a cat*. Unfortunately, the fallacy ensures that the unwary will try to capture this as a *de re* claim about a certain *thing*. But we have seen that this isn't the only way to capture it. That Cicero couldn't be a cat is already guaranteed, on the present theory of names, by the mere *de dicto* necessity of the proposition *that Cicero is not a cat*. Of course I claim that *this* depends on the truth of a *de re* proposition about the incompatibility of two specific *properties*. (The incompatibility claim and the *de dicto* claim are distinct but necessarily equivalent.)

It may help to seal the suggestion that the essentialist's intuitions are thus adequately captured *de dicto*, if we think a little about how essentialists actually promote them. It will help us do this if we momentarily suspend worries about the Fallacy of Reference. Essentialists promote their intuitions by asking us to consider whether we could actually have *Cicero* (or *this table*) and yet have something that was a cat (or made of plastic). Put this way, the appeal is very convincing. When we are asked "Would it really be Cicero?", the rhetorical bite depends on our imagining some cat, in all its feline glory, and somehow intuiting that it *isn't Cicero*.

But if we intuit this, I think we do so only by intuiting that *the properties are all wrong*, not by independently somehow intuiting the failure of an *identity claim*. After all, there's nothing in the thought experiment itself that guarantees the failure of any identity claim *at all*. There's one cat there and it is of course identical with itself. As far as the experiment goes, it may well be identical with Cicero! It isn't a thought experiment in which, say, Cicero is orating to a bored cat. That experiment might well capture the failure of a certain identity claim. But if the present experiment *suggests* the failure of an identity claim, it is only because we are assuming that Cicero must have certain properties, properties that are incompatible with those of the cat. So I think the essentialist's thought experiment cannot work unless it exploits an intuition of the incompatibility of certain *properties*. Thinking that it hinges on direct intuitions about *identity* is a serious, readily understandable, and (nearly) universal error.

For a contrast, suppose the essentialist had instead urged that we "Imagine the aggregation of physical stuff that actually constitutes Cicero (or this table). Could we have that very stuff and yet not have a human being (or a wooden object)?" Not only does this lack "rhetorical bite," it even seems clear that the answer has to be *yes we could*. What makes for the difference is that here we are thinking about the physical stuff independently of the properties we used to pick it out, while in the typical thought experiments we think about it *qua* instantiating those very properties. So I think it is not at all surprising to find that essentialist intuitions are really rooted in the fact that certain properties entail (or are incompatible with) certain other properties.

The Fallacy of Reference encourages us to "identify" *persons*, *tables*, and so on with various mereological sums. In *Naming and Necessity*, Kripke writes:

> *This table* is composed of molecules. Might *it* not have been composed of molecules? Certainly it was a scientific discovery of great moment that *it* was composed of molecules (or atoms). But could anything be *this very object* and not be composed of molecules? Certainly there is some feeling that the answer must be 'no'. At any rate, it's hard to imagine under what circumstances you would have *this very object* and find that *it* is not composed of molecules.[8]

In my view the persuasiveness of this example depends on the fact that Kripke begins by directing our attention to *this table*. For I *do* think that in every world in which that demonstrative denotes anything at all, it denotes something that is not only a table, and not only made of wood, but of course also made of molecules. This is because I think the property of *being this table* entails the property *being made of molecules*.

[8] Kripke (1972, 1980), p. 47, emphasis mine.

But suppose that instead of opening with the words "This table," Kripke had written "The mereological sum that actually happens to be this table." Would the resulting claim have had any plausibility at all? Well, it may be a little harder to imagine a world in which the thing isn't made of molecules than it is to imagine one in which it isn't a table or isn't made of wood, but the principle is the same. In the actual world the regions that absorb the *t*-slices of the object are spatiotemporally connected in a continuous fashion. Imagine a world in which no pair of its *t*-slices are so connected. This is a world in which the very same object exists, but isn't made of molecules. It isn't made of molecules because molecules are things that are temporally extended and occupy connected regions of space-time, and *no* parts of the object in the imagined world have both of these features. This sort of world might not be *physically* possible, and that might make it a little hard to imagine, but I think there can be no doubt about its real possibility.[9]

The best reading of this passage from Kripke thus takes his term "object" as a contextually generated synonym for 'table', rather than taking it as meaning *mereological sum*. This reading makes the claim very persuasive. At least I find it persuasive. And I claim its persuasiveness rests on the entailment mentioned above.

Consider the mereological sum that is in fact the table. It was pretty easy to see that it isn't necessarily a table. It wasn't much harder to see that it isn't necessarily made of wood. It was a little trickier to see that it isn't necessarily made of molecules (or atoms). But I think it is beginning to seem very difficult indeed to find *any* convincing example of a genuinely *de re* necessary truth about that thing that isn't fundamentally *mereological*. But even if there are no such *de re* necessities, this should not be seen as posing a threat to genuine essentialism.

[9] The idea of scattering the *t*-slices was suggested by Richard Healey.

References

Adams, Robert Merrihew 1974. "Theories of Actuality." *Noûs* 8, 211–31.
1981. "Actualism and Thisness." *Synthèse* 49, 3–41.
Almog, J., Perry, J., and Wettstein, H., eds. 1989. *Themes from Kaplan*. New York: Oxford University Press.
Austin, D. F., ed. 1988. *Philosophical Analysis*. Dordrecht: Kluwer Academic Publishers.
Bealer, George 1982. *Quality and Concept*. Oxford: Oxford University Press.
Black, Max 1952. "The Identity of Indiscernibles." *Mind* LXI, 153–64.
Chierchia, G., Partee, B. H., and Turner, R., eds. 1989. *Properties, Types, and Meaning, I*. Dordrecht: Kluwer Academic Publishers.
Chisholm, Roderick 1973. "Parts as Essential to Their Wholes." *Review of Metaphysics* 26, 581–603.
Field, Hartry 1980. *Science without Numbers*. Princeton: Princeton University Press.
Geach, Peter 1967–8. "Identity." *Review of Metaphysics* 21, 3–12.
Gibbard, Alan 1975. "Contingent Identity." *Journal of Philosophical Logic* 4, 187–221.
Goodman, Nelson 1951. *The Structure of Appearance*. Cambridge, Massachusetts: Harvard University Press.
Heller, Mark 1990. *The Ontology of Physical Objects*. Cambridge, England: Cambridge University Press.
Jubien, Michael 1988. "Problems with Possible Worlds," in Austin (1988), 299–322.
1989*a*. "On Properties and Property Theory," in Chierchia, G., Partee, B. H., and Turner, R. (1989), 159–75.
1989*b*. "Straight Talk about Sets." *Philosophical Topics* 17, 91–107.
1991. "Could This Be Magic?" *Philosophical Review* 100, 249–67.
Kaplan, David 1989. "Afterthoughts," in Almog, J., Perry, J., and Wettstein, H. (1989).
Kripke, Saul A. 1972, 1980. *Naming and Necessity*. Cambridge, Massachusetts: Harvard University Press.
Lewis, David 1978. "Truth in Fiction." *American Philosophical Quarterly* 15, 37–46. Reprinted, with postscripts, in Lewis (1983), 261–80.
1983. *Philosophical Papers*, V. 1. New York: Oxford University Press.
1986. *On the Plurality of Worlds*. Oxford: Basil Blackwell.

1991. *Parts of Classes*. Oxford: Basil Blackwell.
Lockwood, Michael 1975. "On Predicating Proper Names." *Philosophical Review* 84, 471–98.
Plantinga, Alvin 1974. *The Nature of Necessity*. New York: Oxford University Press.
1982. "How to be an Anti-Realist." *Proceedings and Addresses of the American Philosophical Association* 55, 47–70.
Putnam, Hilary 1988. *Representation and Reality*. Cambridge, Massachusetts: MIT Press.
Quine, W. V. 1960. *Word and Object*. Cambridge, Massachusetts: MIT Press.
1953, 1961. *From a Logical Point of View*. Cambridge, Massachusetts: Harvard University Press.
Sommers, Fred 1969. "Do We Need Identity?" *Journal of Philosophy* 66, 499–504.
Stalnaker, Robert C. 1984. *Inquiry*. Cambridge, Massachusetts: MIT Press.
1986. "Counterparts and Identity." *Midwest Studies in Philosophy* 11, 121–40.
Thomson, Judith Jarvis 1983. "Parthood and Identity across Time." *Journal of Philosophy* 80, 201–20.
van Inwagen, Peter 1990*a*. "Four-Dimensional Objects." *Noûs* 24, 245–55.
1990*b*. *Material Beings*. Ithaca, New York: Cornell University Press.

Index

For EU product safety concerns, contact us at Calle de José Abascal, 56–1°, 28003 Madrid, Spain or eugpsr@cambridge.org.

www.ingramcontent.com/pod-product-compliance
Ingram Content Group UK Ltd.
Pitfield, Milton Keynes, MK11 3LW, UK
UKHW012339130625
459647UK00009B/386

* 9 7 8 0 5 2 1 1 0 8 5 7 7 *